The

WORKS

of

the Right Honourable Lady

Mary Wortley Montagu

Including

Her Correspondence, Poems and Essays

Volume 5

Elibron Classics
www.elibron.com

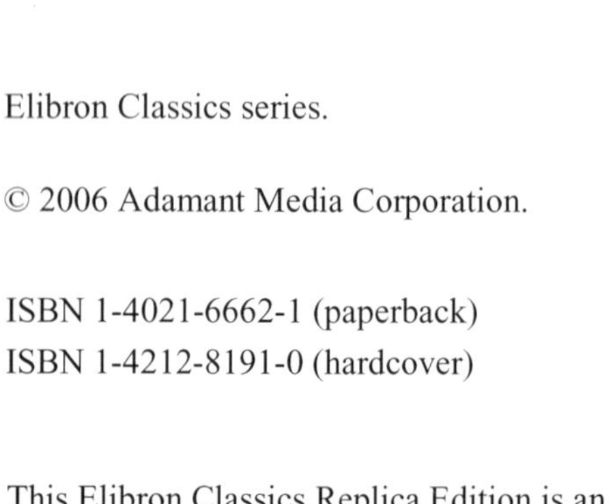

Elibron Classics series.

ISBN 1-4021-6662-1 (paperback)
ISBN 1-4212-8191-0 (hardcover)

This Elibron Classics Replica Edition is an unabridged facsimile of the edition published in 1803 by Richard Phillips, London.

THE

WORKS

OF

THE RIGHT HONOURABLE LADY

MARY WORTLEY MONTAGU.

INCLUDING

HER CORRESPONDENCE, POEMS, AND ESSAYS.

PUBLISHED BY PERMISSION FROM HER GENUINE PAPERS.

IN FIVE VOLUMES.

VOL. V.

LONDON:
PRINTED FOR RICHARD PHILLIPS,
No. 71, St. Paul's Church-yard.

1803.

W. Flint, Printer, Green Arbour Court, St. Sepulchre's.

VOLUME THE FIFTH.

CONTAINING

I. LETTERS TO MR. WORTLEY AND TO THE COUNTESS OF BUTE, DURING HER LAST RESIDENCE ABROAD.

II. POEMS.

III. ESSAYS.

IV. INDEX TO THE FIVE VOLUMES.

LETTERS

DURING

HER LAST RESIDENCE ABROAD.

TO THE COUNTESS OF BUTE.

Louvere, May 30, 1756.

MY DEAR CHILD,

I SENT you a long letter very lately, and enclosed one to Lady Jane. I fear I cannot prevail on Mr. Prescot to take care of my letters; if he should do it, I beg you would be very obliging to him; remember civility costs nothing and buys every thing: your daughters should engrave that maxim in their hearts.

I am sorry Sir William Lowther* died unmarried; he ought to have left some of his breed, which are almost extinct: he died unluckily for his acquaintance, though I think fortunately for himself, being yet ignorant of the ingratitude and vileness of mankind. He knew not what it was to lament misplaced obligations, and thought himself blessed in many friends, whom a short time would have shewn to be worthless, mercenary, designing, scoundrels. The most tender disposition grows callous by miserable experience: I look upon it as the reason, why so many old people leave immense wealth, in a lump, to heirs they neither love nor esteem; and others, like Lord S****n,

* Sir William Lowther, who died in 1756, bequeathed 100,000*l.* in legacies to his several friends with whom he was chiefly associated.

leave it, at random, to they know not who. He was not a covetous man, but had seen so little merit, and was so well acquainted with the vices of mankind, I believe he thought there was none among them deserved any particular distinction. I have passed a long life, and may say, with truth, have endeavoured to purchase friends; accident has put it in my power to confer great benefits, yet I never met with any return, nor indeed any true affection, but from dear Lady Oxford, who owed me nothing. Did not these considerations restrain natural generosity, I am of opinion we should see many Sir William Lowther's; neither is it saying much in favour of the human heart; it is certain that the highest gratification of vanity is found in bestowing; but, when we plainly foresee being exposed by it to insults, nay, perhaps, abuses, which are often liberally dispersed, by those who wish to hide that they are obliged, we abandon the pleasure rather than suffer the consequence. The first shocks, received from this conduct of protesting friends, are felt very severely. I now expect them, and they affect me with no more surprise than rain after sun-shine. The little good I do is scattered with a sparing hand, against my inclination; but I now know the necessisity of managing the hopes of others, as the only links that bind attachment, or even secure us from injuries. Was it possible for me to elevate any body from the station in which they are born, I now would not do it: perhaps it is a rebellion against that providence that has placed them there; all we ought to do is to endeavour to make them easy in the rank assigned them.

I hope you will not forget to send me

the bill of lading, without which I may chance to lose the box, which is very precious to, my dear child,

Your most affectionate mother,

M. WORTLEY.

TO THE COUNTESS OF BUTE.

Venice, Nov. 8, 1756.

DEAR CHILD,

You are extremely good to take so much care of my trifling commissions in the midst of so many important occupations. You judged very right on the subject of Mr. W. I saw him often both at Florence and Genoa, and you may believe I know him. I am not surprised at the character of poor Charles F***'s son. The epithet of *fair* and *foolish* belonged to the whole family; and, as he was over persuaded to marry an ugly woman, I suppose his offspring may have the lost beauty, but retained the folly, in full bloom. Colonel Otway, younger brother to Lady Bridget's spouse, came hither with Lord Mandevile; he told me that she has a daughter with the perfect figure of Lady Winchilsea. I wish she may meet with as good friends as I was to her aunt; but I won't trouble you with old stories. I have, indeed, my head so full of one, that I hardly know what I say about it: I am advised to tell it you, though I had resolved not to do it. I leave it to your prudence to act as you think proper; commonly speaking, silence and neglect are the best answer to defamation, but this is a case so peculiar, that I am persuaded it never happened to any one but myself.

Some few months before Lord William Hamilton married there appeared a foolish song, said to be wrote by a poetical great lady, who I really think was the character of Lady Arabella, in the Female Quixote (without the beauty): you may imagine such a conduct, at court, made him superlatively ridiculous. Lady Delawar, a woman of great merit, with whom I lived in much intimacy, shewed this fine performance to me; we were very merry in supposing what answer Lord William would make to these passionate addresses; she bid me to say something for a poor man, who had nothing to say for himself. I wrote, *extempore*, on the back of the song, some stanzas that went perfectly well to the tune. She promised they should never appear as mine, and faithfully kept her word. By what accident they have fallen into the hands of that thing Dodsley * I know not, but he has

* Dodsley's Collection of Poems was published in three volumes in 1752. The fourth volume appeared in 1755, and the fifth and sixth in 1756. In the sixth volume, p. 230, the dialogue (if it may be so called) between Sir William Young and Lady Mary, is printed, and very erroneously applied.

printed them as addressed, by me, to the last man I should have addressed them to, and my own words as his answer. I do not believe either Job or Socrates ever had such a provocation. You will tell me, it cannot hurt me with any acquaintance I ever had, it is true; but it is an excellent piece of scandal for the same sort of people that propagate, with success, that your nurse left her estate, husband, and family, to go with me to England; and, that then I turned her to starve, after defrauding her of God knows what. I thank God witches are out of fashion, or I should expect to have it deposed, by several credible witnesses, that I had been seen flying through the air on a broomstick, &c.

I am really sick with vexation, but ever your most affectionate mother,

M. WORTLEY.

TO THE COUNTESS OF BUTE.

Padoua, Dec. 28, 1756.

MY DEAR CHILD,

I RECEIVED yours, of November 29th, with great pleasure, some days before I had the box of books, and am highly delighted with the snuff-box: that manufacture is at present as much in fashion at Venice as at London. In general, all the shops are full of English merchandise, and they boast of every thing as coming from London, in the same stile as they used to do from Paris. I was shewn a set of furniture, of their own invention, in a taste entirely new; it consists of eight large armed chairs, the same number of sconces, a table, and prodigious mirror, all of glass. It is impossible to imagine their beauty:

they deserve to be placed in a prince's dressing-room, or grand cabinet; the price demanded is 400*l*. They would be a very proper decoration for the apartment of a prince so young and beautiful as ours.*

The present ministry promises better counsels than have been followed in my time. I am extremely glad to hear the continuation of your father's health, and that you follow his advice. I am really persuaded (without any dash of partiality) no man understands the interest of England better, or has it more at heart. I am obliged to him for whatever he does for you. I will not indulge myself in troubling you with long letters or commissions, when you are charged with so much business at home and abroad; I shall only repeat the Turkish

---

* His present majesty.

maxim, which I think includes all that is necessary in a *court*-life: "The favorites avoid the unfortunate and trust nobody." You may think the second rule illnatured; melancholy experience has convinced me of the ill consequence of mistaking distress for merit; there is no mistake more productive of evil. I could add many arguments to enforce this truth, but will not tire your patience.

I intend to correspond with Lady J. I confess I was much pleased with her little letter; and, supposing Lady M. is commenced fine lady, she may have no leisure to read or answer an old grandmother's letters, I presume Lady J. is to play least in sight till her sister is disposed of: if she loves writing, it may be an employment not disagreeable to herself, and will be extremely grateful to me.

I congratulate my grandaughters on

being born in an age so much enlightened. Sentiments are certainly extremely silly, and only qualify young people to be the bubbles of all their acquaintance. I do not doubt but that the frequency of assemblies has introduced a more enlarged way of thinking. It is a kind of public education, which I have always thought as necessary for girls as boys. A woman, married at five-and-twenty, from under the eye of a strict parent, is commonly as ignorant as she was at five; and no more capable of avoiding the snares, or struggling with the difficulties, she must infallibly meet with in the commerce of the world. The knowledge of mankind (the most useful of all knowledge) can only be acquired by conversing with them. Books are so far from giving that instruction, that they fill the head with a set of wrong notions, from whence springs a trible of Clarissas, Harriets, &c. Yet, such was the method of education when I was in England, which I had it not in my power to correct.

TO THE COUNTESS OF BUTE.

Louvere, June 10, 1757.

It is very true, (my dear child,) we cannot now maintain a family with the product of a flock, though I do not doubt the present sheep afford as much wool and milk as any of their ancestors; and 'tis certain our natural wants are not more numerous than formerly; but the world is past its infancy, and will no longer be contented with spoon meat. Time has added great improvements, but those very improvements have introduced a train of artificial necessities. A collective body of men make a gradual progress in understanding, like that of a single individual. When I reflect on the vast increase of useful, as well as speculative, knowledge the last three hundred years has produced, and that the peasants of this age have more conveniences than the first Emperors of Rome had any notion of, I imagine we are now arrived at that period which answers to fifteen. I cannot think we are older, when I recollect the many palpable follies which are still (almost) universally persisted in: I place that of war as senseless as the boxing of school boys, and whenever we come to man's estate (perhaps a thousand years hence) I do not doubt it will appear as ridiculous as the pranks of unlucky lads. Several discoveries will then be made, and several truths made clear, of which we have now no more idea, than the ancients had of the circulation of the blood, or the optics of Sir Isaac Newton.

You will believe me in a very dull humour when I fill my letter with such whims, and indeed so I am. I have just received the news of Sir J. Gray's departure, and am exceedingly vexed I did not know of his designed journey. I suppose he would have carried my token; * and now I utterly despair of an opportunity of sending it, and therefore enclose a note, on Child, for the value of it.

When you see Lady Rich pray do not fail to present my thanks and compliments. I desire the same to every body that thinks it worth while to inquire after me. You mention a Colonel Rich as her son; I thought he had been killed in Scotland. You see my entire ignorance of all English affairs, and consequently whatever you tell me of my acquaintance has the merit of novelty to me, who correspond with nobody but

* Lady Mary sent a present annually to one of her grandchildren.

yourself and Lady Oxford, whose retirement and ill health does not permit her to send me much news.

I expect a letter of thanks from my grandaughter. I wrote to my grandmother long before her age. I desire you would not see it, being willing to judge of her genius. I know I shall read it with some partiality, which I cannot avoid to all that is yours, as I am your most affectionate mother,

M. WORTLEY.

TO THE COUNTESS OF BUTE.

Padoua, Sept 5, 1757.

I WROTE to you very lately, my dear child, in answer to that letter Mr. Hamilton brought me: he was so obliging to come on purpose from Venice to deliver it, as I believe I told you; but I am so highly delighted with this, dated August 4, giving an account of your little colony, I cannot help setting pen to paper, to tell you the melancholy joy I had in reading it. You would have laughed to see the old fool weep over it. I now find that age, when it does not harden the heart and sour the temper, naturally returns to the milky disposition of infancy. Time has the same effect on the mind as on the face. The predominant passion, the strongest feature, become more conspicuous from the others retiring; the various views of life are abandoned, from want of ability to preserve them, as the fine complexion is lost in wrinkles; but, as surely as a large nose grows larger, and a wide mouth wider, the tender child in your nursery will be a tender old woman, though, perhaps, reason may have restrained the appearance of it, till the mind, relaxed, is no longer capable of concealing its weakness; for weakness it is to indulge any attachment at a period of life when we are sure to part with life itself, at a very short warning. According to the good English proverb, young people may die, but old must. You see I am very industrious in finding comfort to myself in my exit, and to guard, as long as I can, against the peevishness which makes age miserable in itself and contemptible to others. 'Tis surprising to me, that, with the most inoffensive conduct, I should meet enemies, when I cannot be envied for any thing, and have pretensions to nothing.

Is it possible, the old Colonel Duncombe, I knew, should be Lord Feversham, and married to a young wife? As to Lord Ranelagh, I confess it must be a very bitter draught to submit to take his name, but his lady has had a short purgatory, and now enjoys affluence with a man she likes, who I am told is a man of merit, which I suppose she thinks preferable to Lady Selina's nursery. Here are no old people in this country, neither in dress or gallantry. I know only my friend Antonio, who is true to the memory of his adored lady; her picture is always in his sight, and he talks of her in the style of *pastor fido*. I believe I owe his favor to having shewn him her miniature, by Rosalba, which I bought at London: perhaps you remember it in my little collection: he is really a man of worth and sense. Hearing it reported, I need not say by whom, that my retirement was owing to having lost all my money at play, at Avignon, he sent privately for my chief servant, and desired him to tell him naturally if I was in any distress; and not only offered, but pressed, him to lay 3000 sequins on my toilet. I don't believe I could borrow that sum, without good security, among my great relations. I thank God I had no occasion to make use of this generosity; but I am sure you will agree with me, that I ought never to forget the obligation. I could give some other instances, in which he has shown his friendship, in protecting me from mortifications, invented by those that ought to have assisted me; but 'tis a long tiresome story. You will be surprised to hear the general does not yet know these circumstances; he arrived at Venice but a few days before I left it; and, promising me to come to Padoua, at the fair, I thought I should have time sufficient to tell him my history. Indeed, I was in hopes he would have accepted my invitation of lodging in my house; but his multiplicity of affairs hindered him from coming at all. 'Tis only a few days since that he made me a visit, in company with Mr. Hamilton, before whom I did not think it proper to speak my complaints. They are now gone to drink the waters at Vicenza: when they return, I intend removing to Venice, and then shall relate my grievances, which I have more reason to do than ever. I have tired you with this disagreeable subject: I will release you, and please myself in repeating the assurance of my being ever, while I have a being, your most affectionate mother, M. WORTLEY.

My dear child, do not think of reversing nature by making me presents. I would send you all my jewels and my toilet, if I knew how to convey them, though they are in some measure necessary in this country, where it would be, perhaps, reported I had pawned them, if they did not sometimes make their appearance. I know not how to send commissions for things I never saw; nothing of price I would have, as I would not new furnish an inn I was on the point of leaving, for such is this world to me. Though china is in such high estimation here I have sometimes an inclination to desire your father to send me the two large jars, that stood in the windows in Cavendish-square. I am sure he don't value them, and believe they would be of no use to you. I bought them at an auction, for two guineas, before the Duke of Argyle's example had made all china, more or less, fashionable.

TO THE COUNTESS OF BUTE.

Louvere, Sept. 30, 1757.

MY DEAR CHILD,

LORD Bute has been so obliging as to let me know your safe delivery, and the birth of another daughter: may she be as meritorious in your eyes as you are in mine! I can wish nothing better to you both, though I have some reproaches to make you. Daughter! daughter! don't call names; you are always abusing my pleasures, which is what no mortal will bear. Trash, lumber, sad stuff, are the titles you give to my favorite amusement. If I called a white staff a stick of wood, a gold key gilded brass, and the ensigns of illustrious orders coloured strings, this may be philosophically true, but would be very ill received. We have all our playthings; happy are they that can be contented with those they can obtain: those hours are spent in the wisest manner, that can easiest shade the ills of life, and are the least productive of ill consequences. I think my time better employed in reading the adventures of imaginary people, than the Duchess of Marlborough, who passed the latter years of her life in paddling with her will, and contriving schemes of plaguing some, and extracting praise from others, to no purpose; eternally disappointed, and eternally fretting. The active scenes are over at my age. I indulge, with all the art I can, my taste for reading. If I would confine it to valuable books, they are almost as rare as valuable men. I must be content with what I can find. As I approach a second childhood, I endeavour to enter into the pleasures of it. Your youngest son is, perhaps, at this very moment riding on a poker, with great delight, not at all regretting that it is not a gold one, and much less wishing it an Arabian horse, which he could not know how to manage. I am reading an idle tale, not expecting wit or truth in it, and am very glad it is not metaphysics to puzzle my judgement, or history to mislead my opinion: he fortifies his health by exercise; I calm my cares by oblivion. The methods may appear low to busy people; but, if he improves his strength, and I forget my infirmities, we both attain very desirable ends.

I have not heard from your father of a long time. I hope he is well, because you do not mention him.

I am ever, dear child,

Your most affectionate mother,

M. WORTLEY.

TO THE COUNTESS OF BUTE.

Padoua, Oct. 20, 1757.

I AM much obliged to you (my dear child) for the concern you express for me, in yours of July 10th, which I received yesterday, August 20th, but I can assure you I lose very little in not being visited by the English; boys and governors being commonly (not always) the worst company in the world. I am not otherwise affected by it, than as it has an ill appearance in a strange country, though hitherto I have not found any bad effect from it, among my Venetian acquaintance. I was visited, two days ago, by my good friend Cavalier Antonio Mocenigo, who came from Venice to present to me the elected husband of his brother's great grandaughter, who is a noble Venetian, (Signor Zeno,) just of her age, heir to a large fortune, and is one of the most agreeable figures I ever saw; not beautiful, but has an air of so much modesty and good sense, I could easily believe all the good Signor Antonio said of him. They came to invite me to the wedding. I could not refuse such a distinction, but hope to find some excuse before the solemnity, being unwilling to throw away money on fine clothes, which are as improper for me as an embroidered pall for a coffin. But I durst not mention age before my friend, who told me that he is eighty-six. I thought him four years younger; he has all his senses perfect, and is as lively as a man of thirty. It was very pleasing to see the affectionate respect of the young man, and the fond joy that the old one took in praising him.

They would have persuaded me to return with them to Venice; I objected that my house was not ready to receive me; Signor Antonio laughed, and asked me, if I did not think he could give me an apartment, (in truth it was very easy, having five palaces on a row, on the great canal, his own being the centre, and the others inhabited by his relations). I was reduced to tell a fib, (God forgive me,) and pretend a pain in my head; promising to come to Venice before the marriage, which I really intend. They dined here; your health was the first drank; you may imagine I did not fail to toast the bride. She is yet in a convent, but is to be immediately released, and receive visits of congratulation on the contract, till the celebration of the church ceremony, which perhaps may not be this two months; during which time the lover makes a daily visit, and never comes without a present, which custom (at least some times) adds to the impatience of the bridegroom, and very much qualifies that of the lady. You would find it hard to believe a relation of the magnificence, not to say extravagance, on these occasions; indeed it is the only one they are guilty of, their lives in general being spent in a regular handsome economy; the weddings and the creation of a procurator being the only occasions they have of displaying their wealth, which is very great in many houses, particularly this of Mocenigo, of which my friend is the present head. I may justly call him so, giving me proofs of an attachment quite uncommon at London, and certainly disinterested, since I can no way possibly be of use to him. I could tell you some strong instances of it, if I did not remember you have not time to listen to my stories, and there is scarce room on my paper to assure you I am, my dear child,

Your most affectionate mother,

M. WORTLEY.

TO THE COUNTESS OF BUTE.

Venice, Jan. 20, 1758.

I AM always glad to hear of my dear child's health, and daily pray for the continuance of it and all other blessings on you and your family. The carnival hitherto has been clouded by extremely wet weather, but we are in hopes that the sun shine is reserved for the second part of it, when the morning masquerades give all the ladies an opportunity of displaying both their magnificence and their taste, in the various habits that appear at that time. I was very well diverted by them last year. I hear Rome is crammed with Britons, and suppose we shall see them all in their turns. I cannot say that the rising generation gives any general prospect of improvement either in the arts or sciences, or in any thing else. I am exceedingly pleased that the Duchess of Portland is happy in her son-in-law. I must ever interest myself in what happens to any descendant of Lady Oxford. I expect that my books and china should set out, they will be a great amusement to me. I mix so little with the gay world, and at present my garden is quite useless.

Venice is not a place to make a man's fortune in. As for those who have money to throw away, they may do it here more agreeably than in any town I know; strangers being received with great civility, and admitted into all their parties of pleasure. But it requires a good estate and good constitution to play deep and pass so many sleepless nights as is customary in the best company.

I am invited to a great wedding to-morrow, which will be in the most splendid manner, to the contentment of both the families, every thing being equal, even the indifference of the bride and bridegroom, though each of them is extremely pleased, by being set free from governors or governesses. To say truth, I think they are less likely to be disappointed, in the plan they have formed, than any of our romantic couples, who have their heads full of love and constancy.

I stay here, though I am on many accounts better pleased with Padoua. Our great minister, the resident, affects to treat me as one in the opposition. I am inclined to laugh rather than be displeased at his political airs; yet, as I am among strangers, they are disagreeable; and, could I have foreseen them, would have settled in some other part of the world; but I have taken leases of my houses, been at much pains and expense in furnishing them, and am no longer of an age to make long journeys. I saw, some months ago, a countryman of yours, (Mr. Adam,*) who desires to be introduced to you. He seemed to me, in one short visit, to be a man of genius, and I have heard his knowledge of architecture much applauded. He is now in England.

Your account of the changes in ministerial affairs do not surprise me; but nothing could be more astonishing than their all coming in together. It puts me in mind of a friend of mine, who had a large family of favourite animals; and, not knowing how to convey them to his country-house, in separate equipages, he ordered a Dutch mastiff, a cat and

* Mr. Robert Adam, who built Caen-Wood, Luton-Park, &c. and the Adelphi in conjunction with his brother. His designs are published.

her kittens, a monkey, and a parrot, all to be packed up together in one large hamper, and sent by a waggon. One may easily guess how this set of company made their journey; and I have never been able to think of the present compound ministry without the idea of barking, scratching, and screaming. 'Tis too ridiculous a one I own for the gravity of their characters, and still more for the situation the kingdom is in; for, as much as one may encourage the love of laughter, 'tis impossible to be indifferent to the welfare of one's native country.

Adieu! your affectionate mother,

M. WORTLEY.

TO THE COUNTESS OF BUTE.

Venice, April 3, 1758.

MY DEAR CHILD,

SEVERAL English are expected here at the ascension, and I hope to find an opportunity of sending you your pearl necklace. I have been persuaded to take a small house here, as living in lodgings is really very disagreeable. However, I shall still retain my favorite palace at Padoua, where I intend to reside the greater part of the year. In the mean time, I amuse myself with buying and placing furniture, in which I only consult neatness and convenience, having long since renounced (as it is fit I should) all things bordering upon magnificence. I must confess I sometimes indulge my taste in baubles, which is as excuseable in second childhood as in the first. I am sorry the Duchess of Portland has not received my thanks for her obliging letter. I also desire to know the name of the merchant, to whom the duke consigned the legacy left me by Lady Oxford. I see in the newspapers the names of many novels. I do not doubt, but that the greater part of them are trash, lumber, &c. &c.; however, they will serve to kill idle time. I have written you several letters lately; indeed I seldom fail to do it once in a fortnight. Unavoidable visits, together, with the occupation of fitting and furnishing hardly leaves any time to dispose of to my own taste, which is (as it ought to be) more solitary than ever. I left my hermitage, (at Louvere,) that what effects I have might not be dissipated by servants, as they would have been, had I died there.

Sir John Gray was, as I am told, universally esteemed, during his residence here; but alas! he is gone to Naples. I wish the maxims of Queen Elizabeth were received, who always chose men whose birth or behaviour would make the nation respected, people being apt to look upon them as a sample of their countrymen. If those now employed are so --- Lord have mercy upon us! I have seen only Mr. Villette, at Turin, who knew how to support his character. How much the nation has suffered by false intelligence, I believe you are very sensible of; and how impossible it is to obtain truth either from a fool or a knave.

Company forces me upon an abrupt conclusion.

I am ever, my dear child, &c. &c.

M. WORTLEY.

TO THE COUNTESS OF BUTE.

Venice, 1758.

DEAR CHILD,

I RECEIVED yours of the 20th of Feb. yesterday, May the 2d, so irregular is the post. I could forgive the delay, but I cannot pardon the loss of so many that have never arrived at all. Mr. Hamilton is not yet come, nor perhaps will not for some months. I hear he is at Leghorn. General Graham has been dangerously ill; but I am told he is now on his return. We have at present the most extravagant weather that has been known for some years; it is as cold and wet as an English November. Thursday next is the ceremony of the ascension: the show will be entirely spoilt if the rain continues, to the serious affliction of the fine ladies, who all make new clothes on that occasion. We have had lately two magnificent weddings; Lord Mandeville* had the pleasure of dancing at one of them. I appeared at neither, being formal balls, where no masks were admitted, and all people set out in high dress, which I have long renounced, as it is very fit I should; though there were several grandmothers there, who exhibited their jewels.---In this country nobody grows old till they are bedrid.

I wish your daughters to resemble me in nothing but the love of reading, knowing, by experience, how far it is capable of softening the cruelest accidents of life; even the happiest cannot be passed over without many uneasy hours; and there is no remedy so easy

* George, Viscount Mandeville, eldest son of Robert, Duke of Manchester.

as books, which, if they do not give chearfulness, at least restore quiet to the most troubled mind. Those that fly to cards or company for relief generally find they only exchange one misfortune for another.

You have so much business on your hands, I will not take you from more proper employment by a long letter. I am, my dear child, with the warmest affection, ever your tender mother,

M. WORTLEY.

TO THE COUNTESS OF BUTE.

Padoua, July 17, 1758.

MY DEAR CHILD,

I RECEIVED yours last night, which gave me a pleasure beyond what I am able to express, (this is not according to the common expression, but a simple truth). I had not heard from you for some months, and was in my heart very uneasy, from the apprehension of some misfortune in your family; though, as I always endeavour to avoid the anticipation of evil, which is a source of pain, and can never be productive of any good, I stifled my fear as much as possible, yet it cost me many a midnight pang. You have been the passion of my life; you need thank me for nothing; I gratify myself whenever I can oblige you.

How important is the charge of youth! and how useless all the advantages of nature and fortune without a well turned mind! I have lately heard of a very shining instance of this truth, from two gentlemen, (very deserving ones they seem to be,) who have had the curiosity to travel into Muscovy, and now return to England with Mr. Archer. I inquired after my old acquaintance Sir Charles Williams, who I hear is much broken, both in his spirits and constitution. How happy might that man have been, if there had been added to his natural and acquired endowments a dash of morality! If he had known how to distinguish between false and true felicity; and, instead of seeking to encrease an estate already too large, and hunting after pleasures, that have made him rotten and ridiculous, he had bounded his desires of wealth, and followed the dictates of his conscience. His servile ambition has gained him two yards of red ribbon, and an exile into a miserable country, where there is no society and so little taste, that I believe he suffers under a dearth of flatterers. This is said for the use of your growing sons, whom I hope no golden temptations will induce to marry women they cannot love, or comply with measures they do not approve. All the happiness this world can afford is more within reach than is generally supposed. Whoever seeks pleasure will undoubtedly find pain; whoever will persue ease will as certainly find pleasures. The world's esteem is the highest gratification of human vanity; and that is more easily obtained in a moderate fortune than an overgrown one, which is seldom possessed, never gained, without envy. I say esteem; for, as to applause it is a youthful pursuit, never to be forgiven after twenty, and naturally succeeds the childish desire of catching the setting sun, which I can remember running very hard to do; a fine thing truly if it could be caught; but experience soon shew it to be impossible. A wise and honest man lives to his own heart, without that silly splendour that makes him a prey to knaves, and which commonly ends in his becoming one of the fraternity. I am very glad to hear Lord Bute's decent economy sets him above any thing of that kind. I wish it may become national. A collective body of men differs very little from a single man; and frugality is the foundation of generosity. I have often been complimented on the English heroism, who have thrown away so many millions, without any prospect of advantage to themselves, purely to succour a distressed princess. I never could hear these praises without some impatience; they sounded to me like the panegyrics, made by the dependants, on the Duke of Newcastle and poor Lord Oxford, bubbled when they were commended and laughed at when they were undone. Some late events will, I hope, open our eyes: we shall see we are an island, and endeavour to extend our commerce rather than the Quixote reputation, of redressing wrongs and placing diadems on heads that should be equally indifferent to us. When time has ripened mankind into common sense, the name of conquerer will be an odious title. I could easily prove that, had the Spaniards established a trade with the Americans, they would have enriched their country more than by the addition of twenty-two kingdoms, and all the mines they now work --- I do not say possess; since, though they are the proprietors, others enjoy the profit.

My letter is too long; I beg your pardon for it; 'tis seldom I have an opportunity of speaking to you, and I would have you know all the thoughts of your most affectionate mother,

M. WORTLEY.

TO THE COUNTESS OF BUTE.

Padoua, July 14, 1758.

MY DEAR CHILD,

I HOPE this will find you in perfect health. I had a letter from your father last post, dated from Newbold, which tells me a very agreeable piece of news, that the contests of parties, so violent formerly, (to the utter destruction of peace, civility, and common sense,) are so happily terminated, that there is nothing of that sort mentioned in good company. I think I ought to wish you and my grandchildren joy on this general pacification, when I remember all the vexation I have gone through, from my youth upwards, on the account of those divisions, which touched me no more than the disputes between the followers of Mahomet and Ali, being always of opinion that politics and controversy were as unbecoming to our sex as the dress of a prize-fighter; and I would as soon have mounted Fig's theatre as have stewed all night in the gallery of a committee, as some ladies of bright parts have done. Notwithstanding the habitual (I believe I might say natural) indifference, here am I involved in adventures, as surprising as any related in Amadis de Gaul, or even by Mr. Glanville. I can assure you I should not be more surprised at seeing myself riding in the air on a broomstick, than in the figure of a first rate politician. You will stare to hear that your nurse keeps her corner (as Lord Bolingbroke say of Miss Oglethorp) in this illustrious conspiracy. I really think the best head of the junto is an English washer-woman, who has made her fortune with all parties, by her compliance in changing her religion, which gives her the merit of a new convert; and her charitable disposition, of keeping a house of fair reception, for the English captains, sailors, &c. that are distressed, by long sea voyages, (as Sir Samson Legend remarks, in Love for Love,) gains her friends among all public spirited people: the scenes are so comic they deserve the pen of a Richardson to do them justice. I begin to be persuaded the surest way of preserving reputation, and having powerful protectors, is being openly lewd and scandalous. I will not be so censorious, to take examples from my own sex; but you see Doctor Swift, who set at defiance all decency, truth, or reason, had a croud of admirers, and at their head the virtuous and ingenious Earl of Orrery, the polite and learned Mr. Greville, with a number of ladies of fine taste and unblemished characters; while the bishop of Salisbury, (Burnet I mean,) the most indulgent parent, the most generous church-man, and the most zealous asserter of the rights and liberties of his country, was all his life defamed and vilified, and after his death most barbarously calumniated, for having had the courage to write a history without flattery. I knew him in my very early youth, and his condescension, in directing a girl in her studies, is an obligation I can never forget. Appropos of obligations; I hope you remember yours to Lady Knatchbull.* Her only son is here; his father

* Sir Wyndham Knatchbull, of Mersham-Hatch, in Kent, succeeded his father, in 1749, and died, unmarried, September 26, 1763. His mother was Catharine, daughter of James Harris, of Salisbury, Esq.

has been dead nine years; he gave me the first news of it, (so little do I know of what passes amongst my acquaintance.) I made him the bad compliment of receiving him with tears in my eyes, and told him bluntly I was extremely sorry for the loss of so good a friend, without reflecting that it was telling him I was sorry he was in possession of his estate; however, he did not seem offended, but rather pleased at the esteem I expressed for his parents. I endeavoured to repair my blunder by all the civilities in my power, and was very sincere in saying I wished him well, for the sake of his dead and living relations. He appears to me to be what the Duke of Kingston was at Thorsby, though more happy in his guardian and governor. The gentleman who is with him is a man of sense, and I believe has his pupils interest really at heart;

but, there is so much pains taken to make him despise instruction, I fear he will not long resist the alurements of pleasures, which his constitution cannot support.

Here is great joy in the nomination of Mr. Mackenzie for Turin ; his friends hoping to see him on his journey. My token for you lies dormant, and is likely so to do some time. None of the English have visited me, (excepting Sir Wyndham Knatchbull,) or in so cold a way that it would be highly improper to ask favours of them. He is going to Rome; and it may be, I may be obliged to wait till he returns, next ascention, before I have an opportunity of conveying it. Such is the behaviour of my loving countrymen ! in recompense I meet with much friendship amongst the noble Venetians, perhaps the more from being no favourite of a man they dislike. It is the peculiar glory of Mr. Mackenzie that the whole Sardinian court rejoice in the expectation of his arrival, notwithstanding they have been very well pleased with Lord Bristol. To say truth, they are the only young men I have seen abroad, that have found the secret of introducing themselves into the best company. All the others now living here, (however dignified and distinguished,) by herding together, and throwing away their money on worthless objects, have only acquired the glorious title of Golden Asses; and, since the birth of the Italian drama, Goldoni has adorned his scenes with *gli milordi Inglesi,* in the same manner as Moliere represented his Parisian Marquises. If your agreeable brother-in-law is still at London I desire you would wish him joy in my name. If it be no trouble to him, you may take that occasion of sending me some books, particularly two small volumes lately written by Mr. Horace Walpole.* My dear child, I ask your pardon for the intolerable length of this trifling letter. You know age is tatling, and something should be forgiven to the sincere affection with which I am ever,

Your most affectionate mother,

M. WORTLEY.

---

* Royal and Noble Authors, 8vo. 1758.

TO THE COUNTESS OF BUTE.

Venice, Oct. 10, 1758.

DEAR CHILD,

I AM sorry for the death of Lord Carlisle.* He was my friend as well as acquaintance; a man of uncommon probity and good nature. I thank you for your kind intention of sending me books, but let there be no more duplicates. As well as I love nonsense, I do not desire to have the same twice over --- no translations --- no periodical papers --- though I confess some of the "World" entertain me very much, particularly Lord Chesterfield and Horry Walpole; but, whenever I met Dodsley

* He died September 4, 1758.

I wished him *out of the world*, with all my heart. The title was a very lucky one, being, as you see, productive of puns; "*world without end*," which is all the species of wit some people can either practice or understand. Smith * has lately named Murray's † sister, a beauteous virgin of forty, who, after having refused all the peers in England, because the niecety of her conscience would not permit her to give her hand when her heart was untouched, remained without a husband till the charms of that fine gentleman deter-

---

* Joseph Smith, Esq. consul at Venice. He made a large collection of pictures and gems, which were purchased by his present majesty for 20,000*l.* The "Dactyliotheca Smithiana," in 2 vol. 4to. was published in 1765.

† Mr. Murray was afterward ambassador at the Porte, and died, in the Lazaretto, at Venice, in 1777, upon his return to England.

mined her to change her condition, who is only eighty-two. In short, they are, as Lord Orrery says of Swift and company, "an illustrious groupe." I should be sorry to offend a man of such strict honour as Lord H***ssc, who, like a great politician, has provided for a worthless relation, without expense. It has long been a maxim not to consider if a man be fit for a place, but if the place be fit for him; and we see the fruits of these Machiavelian proceedings.

I was well acquainted with Mr. Walpole, at Florence, and indeed he was particularly civil to me. I am encouraged to ask a favour of him, if I did not know, that few people have so good memories as to remember, so many years backwards as have passed since I have seen him. If he has treated the character of Queen Elizabeth with disrespect all the women should tear him in pieces, for abusing the glory of her sex.* Neither is it just to put her in the list of authors having never published any thing, though we have Mr. Camden's authority, that she wrote many valuable pieces, chiefly translations from the Greek. I wish all monarchs would bestow their leisure hours on such studies --- perhaps they would not be very useful to mankind; but, it may be asserted, as a certain truth, that their own minds would be more improved than by the amusements of Quadrille or Cavagnole.

I desire you would thank your father for the china jars; if they arrive safely they will do me great honour in this

---

* Alluding to the character of Queen Elizabeth, in his Royal and Noble Authors.

country. The patriarch died here lately. He had a large temporal estate; and, by long life and extreme parsimony, has left four hundred thousand sequins in his coffers, which is inherited by two nephews; and I suppose will be dissipated as scandalously as it was accumulated. The town is full of faction, for the election of his successor; and the ladies are always very active on these occasions. I have observed that they have ever had more influence in republics than in a monarchy. 'Tis true, a king has often a powerful mistress, but she is governed by some male favourite. In commonwealths, votes are easily acquired by the fair; and she, who has most beauty or art, has a great sway in the senate. I run on troubling you with stories very insignificant to you, and taking up your time, which

I am very certain is taken up in matters of more inportance than my old wives tales. My dear child, God bless you and yours. I am, with the warmest sentiments of my heart, your most affectionate mother,

M. WORTLEY.

TO THE COUNTESS OF BUTE.

Padoua, Nov. 19, 1758.

MY DEAR CHILD,

I AM glad to hear Lady Betty Mackenzie is so amiable. I have dined with her at the Duke of Argyll's, and seen her several times, but she was then of an age, when young ladies think silence becoming in the presence of their parents. Lady Mary,* hardly passed her childhood, was more free, and I confess was my favourite in the family. The rejoicings in this town, for the election of the Pope,† who was archbishop of this city, are not yet over, and have been magnificent to the last degree;

* Lady Mary Coke.

† Cardinal Lambertine, Benedict XIV.

the illuminations, fire-works, and assemblies, have been finer than any known of many years. I have had no share in them, going to bed at the hour they begun. --- It is remarkable that the present Pope* has his mother still living, at Venice; his father died only last winter. If he follows the steps of his predecessor, he will be a great blessing to his dominions. I could, with pleasure to myself, enlarge on the character of the deceased prelate, which was as extraordinary as that of the Czar Peter, being equally superior to the prejudices of education, but you would think me bribed by the civilities I received from him. I had the honour of a most obliging message, by his particular order, the post before that which brought news of his death.

* Cardinal Rezzonico, Clement XIII.

Lord Carlisle was the most intimate friend of my father; they were of the same age, and, if he had not been dedicated to retirement, would have been one of Duke of Kingston's guardians; and I firmly believe would have acted in a different manner from those who were intrusted, being (with all his failings) a man of great honour.

I am very glad to hear of your father's health; mine is better than I ought to expect at my time of life. I believe Mr. Anderson talks partially of me, as to my looks; I know nothing of the matter, as it is eleven years since I have seen my figure in a glass, and the last reflection I saw there was so disagreeable, that I resolved to spare myself such mortifications for the future, and shall continue that resolution to my life's end. To indulge all pleasing amusements, and avoid all images that give disgust, is in my opinion the best method to attain or confirm health.---I ought to consider yours, and shorten my letter, while you are in a condition that makes reading uneasy to you.

God bless you and yours, my dear child, is the most ardent wish of your affectionate mother,

M. WORTLEY.

TO MR. WORTLEY.

Venice, Dec. 11, 1758.

I ASSURE you I live as agreeably here as any stranger in my circumstances possibly can do; and, indeed, a repetition of all the civilities I have received here would sound more like vanity than truth. I am sensible that I owe a great part of them to Grimani, who is in the first esteem and authority in this republic; and, as he takes pains to appear my friend, his relations and allies, of both sexes, (who are the most considerable people here,) endeavour to oblige me in all sorts of ways. The carnival is expected to be more brilliant than common, from the great concourse of noble strangers. The Princess of Holstein and the Prince of Wolfenbuttle (nephew of the Empress) are already arrived, and the Electoral Prince of Saxony is expected next week. If my age and humour would permit me much pleasure in public amusements, here are a great variety of them. I take as little share of them as I can.

> "Frui paratis et valido mihi
> Latöe dones, et precor integrâ
> Cum mente, nec turpem senectam
> Degere, nec citharâ carentem."
>
> HOR. OD. L. 1. O. 31.

You see I have got a Horace, which is borrowed of the consul, who is a good scholar; but I am very impatient for my own books. I could wish you to send me the cushions that were used at Constantinople; they would be very useful to me here. As to what regards ------- I have long since fixed my opinion concerning him. Indeed, I am not insensible of the misfortune, but I look upon it as the loss of a limb, which should cease to give solicitude by being irretievable.

Lord Brudenel * is here, and appears to be in an extremely bad state of health, and unwilling to return to England, being apprehensive of the air. I fear his friends will have the affliction of losing him, as he seems highly disposed, if not actually fallen into a consumption. I have had a letter from Mr. Mackenzie, who is excessively liked at Turin. I cannot contrive to go there, but heartily wish I could contrive to see him and Lady Betty in some other place. I am determined, on account of my health, to take some little jaunt next spring; perhaps on the side of the Tyrol, which I have never seen, but hear it is an ex-

* John, Lord Brudenel, eldest son of George, Earl of Cardigan.

ceedingly fine country. To say truth, I am tempted by the letters of Lady F. Stewart and Sir James. I never new people more to my taste. They reside in a little town, only two days journey from Padoua, where it will be easy to find a lodging for the summer months, and I am sure of being pleased in their company. I have found, wherever I have travelled, that the pleasantest spots of ground have been in the vallies, which are encompassed with high mountains.

TO THE COUNTESS OF BUTE.

Venice, Feb. 21, 1759.

MY DEAR CHILD,

If half of the letters I have sent to you have reached you, I believe you think I have always a pen in my hand; but, I am really so uneasy, by your long silence, I cannot forbear inquiring the reason of it, by all the methods I can imagine. My time of life is naturally inclined to fear; and though I resist (as well as I can) all the infirmities incident to age, I feel but too sensibly the impressions of melancholy, when I have any doubt of your welfare. You fancy, perhaps, that the public papers give me information enough; and, that when I do not see in them any misfortune of yours, I ought to conclude you have none. I can assure you I never see any, excepting by accident. Our resident has not the good breeding to send them to me; and, after having asked for them once or twice, and being told they were engaged, I am unwilling to demand a trifle at the expense of thanking a man who does not desire to oblige me; indeed, since the ministry of Mr. Pitt, he is so desirous to signalize his zeal for the contrary faction, he is perpetually saying ridiculous things, to manifest his attachment; and, as he looks upon me (nobody knows why) to be the friend of a man I never saw, he has not visited me once this winter. The misfortune is not great. I cannot help laughing at my being mistaken for a politician. I have often been so, though I ever thought politics so far removed from my sphere. I cannot accuse myself of dabling in them, even when I heard them talked over in all companies; but, as the old song says:

> Tho' through the wide world we should range
> 'Tis in vain from our fortune to fly.

I forget myself and tattle on, without remembering you are too much employed to throw away time on reading insignificant letters; you should however forgive them, in consideration of the real affection of your very loving mother,

M. WORTLEY.

TO MR. WORTLEY.

Venice, Feb. 24, 1759.

I RETURN you many thanks for yours of the 5th instant. I never have received any in so short a time from England. I am very sincerely, heartily, glad to hear of your health, but will not trouble you with reading a long letter, which may be uneasy to you, when I write so often and fully to our daughter. I have not heard from her of some time; I hope her silence is not occasioned by any indisposition. I hear her and her family praised very much by every Briton that arrives here. I need not say what comfort I receive from it. It is now finer weather than I ever saw in the season, (Naples excepted); the sun shines with as much warmth as in May. I walk in my little garden every morning. I hope you do the same at Bath.

The carnival is now over, and we have no more ridotto or theatrical amusements. Diversions have taken a more private, perhaps, a more agreeable, turn here. It is the fashion to have little houses of retreat, where the lady goes every evening, at seven or eight o'clock, and is visited by all her intimates of both sexes, which commonly amount to seventy or eighty persons, where they have play, concerts of music, sometimes dancing, and always a handsome collation. I believe you will think these little assemblies very pleasing; they really are so. Whoever is well acquainted with Venice must own that it is the centre of pleasure; not so noisy, and, in my opinion, more refined than Paris. The young Earl of Northampton* is now at Florence, and was here in the carnival. He is lively and good natured, with what is called a pretty figure. I believe he is of a humour likely to fall in love with many; the first agreeable girl he meets with in London. I send this by a gentleman who is just returned from making a very extraordinary journey. I dined with him yesterday at General Graham's. He is a sensible man, and gives a good account of his plan. Almost all books are either defective or fabulous. I have observed, that the only true intelligence of distant countries is to be had from those who have passed them, without a design of publishing their remarks.

---

* He married Lady Anne Somerset, eldest daughter of Charles Noel, Duke of Beaufort.

TO THE COUNTESS OF BUTE.

Venice, May 22, 1759.

MY DEAR CHILD,

I AM always pleased to hear from you, but particularly so when I have any occasion of congratulation. I sincerely wish you joy of your infants having gone happily through the small pox. I had a letter from your father before he left London. He does not give so good an account of his spirits as you do, but I hope his journeys will restore them. I am convinced nothing is so conducive to health and absolutely necessary to some constitutions. I am not surprised as I believe you think I ought to be, at Lord L***r's leaving his large estate to his lady, notwithstanding the contempt with which he always treated her, and her real inability of managing it. I expect you should laugh at me, for the exploded notion of predestination, yet I confess I am inclined to be of the opinion, that nobody makes their own marriage or their own will: it is what I have often said to the Duchess of Marlborough, when she has been telling me her last intentions, none of which she has performed; chusing Lord Chesterfield for her executor, whose true character she has many times enlarged upon. I could say much more to support this doctrine, if it would not lengthen my letter beyond a readable size.

Building is the general weakness of old people; I have had a twitch of it myself, though certainly it is the highest absurdity, and as sure a proof of doatage as pink coloured ribands, or even matrimony. Nay, perhaps, there is more to be said in defence of the last: I mean in a childless old man; he may prefer a boy born in his own house, though he knows it is not his own, to disrespectful or worthless nephews or neices. But there is no excuse for beginning an edifice he can never inhabit, or probably see finished. The Duchess of Marlborough used to ridicule the vanity of it, by saying one might always live upon other peoples follies: yet you see she built the most ridiculous house I ever saw, since it really is not habitable, from the excessive damps; so true it is, the things that we would do, those do we not, and the things we would not do, those do we daily. I feel in myself a proof of this assertion, being much against my will at Venice, though I own it is the only great town where I can properly reside, yet here I find so many vexations, that, in spite of all my philosophy, and (what is more powerful,) my phlegm, I am oftner out of humour than among my plants, and poultry in the country. I cannot help being concerned at the success of iniquitous schemes, and grieve for oppressed merit. You, who see these things every day, think me as unreasonable, in making them matter of complaint, as if I seriously lamented the change of seasons. You should consider I have lived almost a hermit ten years, and the world is as new to me as to a country girl transported from Wales to Coventry. I know I ought to think my lot very good, that can boast of some sincere friends among strangers.

Sir Wyndham Knatchbull and his governor, Mr. de Vismes, are at length parted. I am very sorry for them both. I cannot help wishing well to the young man, who really has merit, and would have been happy in a companion that sincerely loved him and studied his interest.

My letter is so long I am frighted at it myself. I never know when to end when I write to you. Forgive it amongst the other infirmities of your affectionate mother,

M. WORTLEY.

TO THE COUNTESS OF BUTE.

Padoua, June 14, 1759.

MY DEAR CHILD,

I HAVE this minute received yours of May 24. I am glad the little picture pleases Lady Mary. It is a true representation of the summer dishabille of the Venetian ladies. I could heartily wish to see your brother-in-law and Lady Betty Mackenzie, and fancy that I have a thousand questions to ask them, in relation to their nephews and neices. Whatever touches you is important to me. I fear I must not expect that satisfaction, as they are obliged to reside at Turin; and I cannot resolve to appear in a court, where old people always make an ill figure, even though they may have business there.

Lord Fordwich* is arrived here; he made me a visit yesterday, and appears a well-disposed youth. Lord Brudenel continues here, and seems to have no desire to revisit his native land. I suppose you are now at Kew, with all your rising family around you: may they ever be blessings to you! I believe you who see them every day scarcely think more of them than I do.

This town is at present very full of company, though the opera is not much applauded. I have not yet seen it, nor do I intend to break my rest for its sake; it being about the hour I go to sleep. I continue my college-hours, by which custom I am excluded from many fashionable amusements; but, in recompense, I have better health and spirits than many younger ladies, who pass

* The late Earl Cowper.

their nights at the ridotto, and days in spleen for their losses there. Play is the general plague of Europe. I know no corner of it entirely free from the infection. I do not doubt but that the familiarities of the gaming-table contribute very much to that decay of politeness of which you complain; for the pouting and quarrels, which naturally arise from disputes there, must put an end to all complaisance, or even good will towards each other. If they plead necessity it is one proof among many that no one should trust their virtue to necessity, the force of which is never known till it is felt; and, it is therefore one of our first duties to avoid the temptation of it. I am not pleading for avarice --- far from it. A prudential care of ones own affairs, or, to go farther, a desire to be in circumstances to do good to ones friends is not only excusable, but highly laudable; never blamed but by those who would persuade others to throw away their money, in hopes to pick up a share of it. The greatest declaimers for disinterestedness, I have ever known, have been themselves capable of the vilest actions, on the least view of profit; and the greatest instances of true generosity given by those who were regular in their expenses, and superior to the vanities in fashion. I believe you are tired of my dull moralities, but I confess I am in low spirits. My blessing to yours.

M. WORTLEY.

TO THE COUNTESS OF BUTE.

Padoua, Aug. 10, 1759.

MY DEAR CHILD,

SINCE you tell me my letters (such as they are) are agreeable to you, I shall, for the future, indulge myself in thinking upon paper, when I write to you. There are preparations, at Venice, for a regatta: it can hardly be performed till the middle of next month. I shall remove thither to see it, though I have already seen that which was exhibited in compliment to the Prince of Saxony. It is by far the finest sight in Europe, (not excepting our own coronations,) and it is hardly possible to give you a just notion of it, by description. General Graham has shewn me a letter from Lord Bute, very obliging to me, and which gives a very good impression both of his head and heart, from the honest resolutions and just reflections that are in it. My time here is intirely employed in riding, walking, and reading. I see little company, not being in a humour to join in their diversions. I feel greatly the loss of Sir James Stuart and Lady Fanny, whose conversation was equally pleasing and instructive. I do not expect to have it soon replaced, as there are few such couples. One of my best friends, at Venice, I believe your father remembers. He is Signor Antonio Mocenigo, widower of that celebrated beauty, the Procuratessa Mocenigo, and is eighty-two, in perfect health and spirits. His eloquence is much admired in the senate, where he has great weight. He still retains a degree of that figure, which once made him esteemed as one of the handsomest men in the republic. I am particularly proud of being admitted into the number of seven or eight friends, nearly of his own age, who pass their evenings with him.

I was as well acquainted with ——'s *two first* wives, as the great difference of our ages permitted, and I fancy they have both broken their hearts, by being chained to such a companion. 'Tis really terrible for a well-bred virtuous young woman to be confined to the conversation of the object of her contempt. There is but one thing to be done in that case, which is a method I am sure you have observed practised, by some ladies, with success. I need not name that they associate the husband with the lap-dog, and manage so, that they make just the same figure in the family. My lord and *Dell* tag after madam to all indifferent places, and stay at home together whenever she goes into company where they would be troublesome.

Compliments to Lord Bute. I am to you both an affectionate mother,

M. WORTLEY.

TO THE COUNTESS OF BUTE.

Genoa, Dec. 8, 1759.

MY DEAR CHILD,

I RECEIVED yours, of October 24, yesterday, which gave me great pleasure, by the account of the good health of you and yours; I need not say how near that is to my heart. I had the satisfaction of an entertaining letter from your father, out of Germany, by which I find he has had both benefit and amusement from his travels. I hope he is now with you.

I find you have many wrong notions of Italy, which I do not wonder at. You can take your ideas of it only from books or travellers; the first are generally antiquated or confined to trite observations, and the other yet more superficial; they return no more instructed than they might have been at home, by the help of a map. The boys only remember where they met with the best wine or the prettiest women; and the governors (I speak of the most learned amongst them) have only remarked situations and distances, or, at most, státues and edifices, as every girl that can read a French novel, and boy that can construe a scene in Terence, fancies they have attained to the French and Latin languages, when, God knows, it requires the study of a whole life to acquire a perfect knowledge of either of them: so, after a tour (as they call it) of three years, round Europe, people think themselves qualified to give exact accounts of the customs, politics, and interests of the dominions they have gone through post; when a very long stay, a diligent inquiry, and a nice observation are requisite even to a moderate degree of knowing a foreign country, especially here, where they are naturally very reserved. France indeed is more easily seen through; the French always talking of themselves, and the government being the same, there is little difference from one province to another; but, in Italy, the different laws make different customs and manners. There are many things very particular here, from the singularity of the government; some of which I do not care to touch upon, and some are still in use here, though obsolete in almost all other places, as the estates of all the great families, being unalienable, as they were formerly in England. This would have made them very potent, if it were not balanced by another law, that divides whatever land the father dies possessed of among all the sons, the eldest having no advantage, but the finest house and best furniture, which occasions numerous branches and few large fortunes, with a train of consequences you may imagine. But I cannot let pass in silence the prodigious alteration, since Misson's writing, in regard to our sex. This reformation (or, if you please, depravation) begun so lately as the year 1732, when the French over-run this part of Italy, but it has been carried on with such fervor and success, that the Italians go far beyond their patterns, the Parisian ladies, in the extent of their liberty. I am not so much surprised at the women's conduct, as I am amazed at the change in the men's sentiments. Jealousy, which was once a point of honour among them, is exploded to that degree, that it is become the most infamous and ridiculous of all characters; and you cannot more affront a gentleman, than to suppose him capable of it. Divorces are also introduced, and frequent enough they have long been in fashion in Genoa; several of the finest and greatest ladies there having two husbands alive.

I am afraid you will think this a long letter; but you tell me that you are without company, and in solitude, though yours appears to me to be a sort of paradise. You have an agreeable habitation, a pleasant garden, a man you love and who loves you, and are surrounded with a numerous and hopeful progeny. May they all prove comforts to your age! That and all other blessings are daily wished for you by, my dear child,

Your affectionate mother,

M. WORTLEY.

TO THE COUNTESS OF BUTE.

Venice, March 18, 1760.

MY DEAR CHILD,

I AM afraid some letters both of yours and mine are lost, nor am I much surprised at it, seeing the managements here. In this world much must be suffered, and we ought all to follow the rule of Epictetus, "Bear and forbear" General Wolfe * is to be lamented, but not pitied. I am of your opinion, that compassion is only owing to his mother and intended bride, who I think the greater sufferer, (however sensible I am of a parents tenderness). Disappointments in youth are those which are felt

* General Wolfe was killed, at the siege of Quebec, September 16, 1759.

with the greatest anguish, when we are all in expectation of happiness, perhaps not to be found in this life. I am very much diverted with the adventures of the three graces who are coming to London, and am heartily sorry their mother has not learning enough to write memoirs. She might make the fortune of half a dozen Dodsleys. The youngest girl (called here *Bettina*) is taller than the Duchess of Montagu, and as red and white as any German alive. If she has sense enough to follow good instructions, she will be irresistible, and may produce very glorious novelties. Our great minister has her picture in his collection — *basta!*

My health is better than I can reasonably expect at my age, but my life is so near a conclusion, that where or how I pass it (if innocently) is almost become indifferent to me. I have outlived the greatest part of my acquaintance; and, to say the truth, a return to crowd and bustle, after my long retirement, would be disagreeable to me. Yet, if I could be of use either to your father or your family, I would venture the shortening the insignificant days of your affectionate mother,

M. WORTLEY.

TO THE COUNTESS OF BUTE.

Venice, Nov. 6, 1760.

MY DEAR CHILD,

I AM afraid you will think me very troublesome, and that I do not enough consider the various duties you are now obliged to. Indeed I am thoroughly sensible you have little time to throw away, but I am (privately) solicited to mention a thing to you, which, in my opinion, I ought not to omit.

The senate have appointed two procurators of St. Mark to compliment his majesty on his accession. They are of the first families here, Contarini and Morosini, and are neither of them married. Madam Capello has been so ridiculous, both at London and Rome, that I believe they will not often send ambassadresses. These cavaliers are of such a character as will do honour to their country: they are vastly rich, and desirous to shew their magnificence in the court of England. They apprehend (I know not why) that they shall be thanked and not permitted to come. I am far from a politician, God knows, but it seems to me, both in public and private life, civilities should never be refused, when they are sincerely meant as proofs of respect. I have no personal interest in this affair, nor can receive any advantage from their embassy, but an opportunity of sending some trifles to my grandaughter, which I hoped to do by Lord Titchfield,* who has been long at Turin. I am now told he will not take Venice in his road, when he returns to London.

---

* The present Duke of Portland.

I am sorry to tell you I fear General Graham is in a declining state of health. I suppose you know poor Mr. Hamilton is at Petersburgh. I am ever, my dear child,

Your most affectionate mother,

M. WORTLEY.

TO THE COUNTESS OF BUTE.

Venice, Nov. 18, 1760.

MY DEAR CHILD,

THE three fine ladies I mentioned set out for London three days ago. The fathers name was W * ne, of Yorkshire, and the Signora Madre is a Greek, and, I believe, once remarkably handsome. I should have said much more about them, if you had been at Caen-Wood, and in full leisure to read novels. The story deserves the pen of my dear Smollett, who, I am sorry, disgraces his talent by writing those stupid romances, commonly called history. Shebbeare does yet worse and dabbles in filthy politics, instead of making more Lydias for my entertainment.

I thank God I can live here in a quiet

retirement. I am very far from any view beyond tranquillity; and if I have been so much vexed at M * * 's behaviour, I desire not his ruin. I am told he gives political reasons for his conduct towards me, which, if true, I ought to pardon him by all the maxims of modern ethics.

I give you thanks for your information of the death of the King. You may imagine how I am affected by it, but I will not trouble you at this time with a long letter.

My health is very precarious; may yours long continue, and the prosperity of your family. I bless God that I have lived to see you so well established, and am ready to sing my "Nunc dimittis" with pleasure.

My dear child, I am ever,

Your affectionate mother,

M. WORTLEY.

POEMS

OF THE RIGHT HONORABLE

Lady MARY WORTLEY MONTAGU.

PRINTED FROM HER ORIGINAL MANUSCRIPTS.

POEMS.

JULIA TO OVID.

WRITTEN AT TWELVE YEARS OF AGE, IN IMITATION OF OVID'S EPISTLES.

ARE love and power incapable to meet?
And must they all be wretched who are great?
Enslav'd by titles, and by forms confin'd,
For wretched victims to the state design'd.

What rural maid that my sad fortune knows
Would quit her cottage to embrace my woes?
Would be this cursed sacrifice to power,
This wretched daughter of Rome's Emperour?
When sick with sighs to absent Ovid given,
I tire with vows the unrelenting Heaven.
Drown'd in my tears, and with my sorrows pale,
What then do all my kindred gods avail?

Let proud Augustus the whole world subdue,
Be mine to place all happiness in you;
With nobler pride I can on thrones look down,
Can court your love, and can despise a crown.—

Oh Love! thou pleasure never dearly bought!
Whose joys exceed the very lover's thought;
Of that soft passion, when you teach the art,
In gentle sounds, it steals into the heart.
With such sweet magic does the soul surprize,
'Tis only taught us better by your eyes.

Oh, Ovid! first of the inspir'd train,
To Heaven I speak in that enchanting strain,
So sweet a voice can never plead in vain.
Apollo will protect his favorite son,
And all the little Loves unto thy succour run.
The Loves and Muses, in thy prayer shall join,
And all their wishes and their vows be thine;
Some God will soften my hard Father's breast,
And work a miracle to make thee blest.

* * * * * * * * * * * *

* * * * * * * * * * * *

Hard as this is, I even this could bear,
But greater ills than what I feel I fear,
My fame, my Ovid, both for ever fled,
What greater evil is there left to dread?
Yes, there is one — — — — — —
Avert it, Gods, who do my sorrows see!
Avert it, thou who art a God to me!
When back to Rome your wishing eyes are cast,
And on the lessening towers you gaze your last—
When fancy shall recall unto your view
The pleasures now for ever lost to you,
The shining court, and all the thousand ways,
To melt the nights and pass the happy days—
Will you not sigh, and hate the wretched maid,
Whose fatal love your safety has betray'd?
Say that from me your banishment does come,
And curse the eyes that have expell'd you Rome?
Those eyes which now are weeping for your woes,
The sleep of death shall then for ever close.

IRREGULAR VERSES TO TRUTH.

WRITTEN AT FOURTEEN YEARS OF AGE.

WHERE, lovely Goddess, dost thou dwell?
In what remote and silent shade?
Within what cave or lonely cell?
With what old hermit, or unpractised maid?
In vain I've sought thee all around,
But thy unfashionable sound
In crowds was never heard,
Nor ever has thy form in town or court appear'd.

The sanctuary is not safe to thee,
Chas'd thence by endless mystery;
Thy own professors chase thee thence,
And wage eternal war with thee and sense;
Then in perplexing comments lost,
E'en when they would be thought to shew thee most.
Most beautiful when most distress'd,
Descend, Oh Goddess, to my breast;
There thou may'st reign, unrival'd and alone,
My thoughts thy subjects, and my heart thy throne!

SONG.

HOW happy is the harden'd heart,
Where interest is the only view!
Can sigh and meet, or smile and part,
Nor pleas'd, nor griev'd, nor false, nor true—
Yet have they truly peace of mind?
Or do they ever truly know
The bliss sincerer tempers find
Which truth and virtue can bestow?

THE LADY'S RESOLVE.

WRITTEN ON A WINDOW, SOON AFTER HER MARRIAGE, 1713.

WHILST thirst of praise, and vain desire of
fame
In every age, is every woman's aim;
With courtship pleas'd, of silly toasters proud,
Fond of a train, and happy in a crowd;
On each proud fop bestowing some kind glance,
Each conquest owing to some loose advance;
While vain coquets affect to be pursu'd,
And think they're virtuous, if not grossly lewd:
Let this great maxim be my virtue guide;
In part she is to blame that has been try'd—
He comes too near that comes to be deny'd.

TOWN ECLOGUES.*

WRITTEN IN THE YEAR, 1715.

MONDAY.

ROXANA; OR, THE DRAWING-ROOM.

ROXANA from the Court retiring late,
Sigh'd her soft sorrows at St. James's gate.
Such heavy thoughts lay brooding in her breast,
Not her own chairmen with more weight oppress'd;
They groan the cruel load they're doom'd to bear;
She in these gentle sounds express'd her care.

"Was it for this, that I these roses wear?
For this new-set the jewels for my hair?
Ah! princess!† with what zeal have I pursu'd!
Almost forgot the duty of a prude.

* Written as a Parody upon the Pastorals of Pope and Philips, which had then their full share of fame. The same idea was afterward pursued by C. Jenner, and his Town Eclogues are printed in Dodsley's Collection.

† The Princess of Wales, afterward Queen Caroline.

Thinking I never could attend too soon,
I've miss'd my prayers, to get me dress'd by n oon
For thee, ah! what for thee, did I resign?
My pleasures, passions, all that e'er was mine.
I sacrific'd both modesty and ease,
Left operas and went to filthy plays;
Double entendres shock my tender ear;
Yet even this for thee I chose to bear.
In glowing youth, when nature bids be gay,
And every joy of life before me lay,
By honour prompted, and by pride restrain'd,
The pleasures of the young my soul disdain'd:
Sermons I sought, and with a mien severe
Censur'd my neighbours, and said daily pray'r.

"Alas! how chang'd—with the same sermon-mien
That once I pray'd, the *What-d'ye-call't* * I've seen.
Ah! cruel princess, for thy sake I've lost
That reputation which so dear had cost:
I, who avoided every public place,
When bloom and beauty bade me show my face;

* A Farce, by Gay.

Now near thee constant every night abide
With never-failing duty by thy side,
Myself and daughters standing on a row,
To all the foreigners a goodly show!
Oft had your drawing-room been sadly thin,
And merchant's wives close by the chair been seen;
Had not I amply fill'd the empty space,
And sav'd your Highness from the dire disgrace.

"Yet Coquetilla's artifice prevails,
When all my merit and my duty fails:
That Coquetilla, whose deluding airs
Corrupts our virgins, and our youth ensnares;
So sunk her character, so lost her fame,
Scarce visited before your Highness came:
Yet for the bed-chamber 'tis her you chuse,
When Zeal and Fame and Virtue you refuse.
Ah! worthy choice! not one of all your train
Whom censure blasts not, and dishonours stain.
Let the nice hind now suckle dirty pigs,
And the proud pea-hen hatch the cuckoo's eggs!

Let Iris leave her paint and own her age,
And grave Suffolka wed a giddy page!
A greater miracle is daily view'd,
A virtuous princess with a court so lewd.

"I know thee, Court! with all thy treach'rous wiles,
Thy false caresses and undoing smiles!
Ah! Princess, learn'd in all the courtly arts
To cheat our hopes, and yet to gain our hearts!

"Large lovely bribes are the great statesman's aim;
And the neglected patriot follows fame.
The prince is ogled; some the king pursue;
But your Roxana only follows you.
Despis'd Roxana, cease, and try to find
Some other, since the Princess proves unkind:
Perhaps it is not hard to find at court,
If not a greater, a more firm support."

TUESDAY.

ST. JAMES'S COFFEE-HOUSE.

SILLIANDER AND PATCH.

THOU, who so many favours hast receiv'd,
Wond'rous to tell, and hard to be believ'd,
Oh! Hervey*, to my lays attention lend,
Hear how two lovers boastingly contend:
Like thee successful, such their bloomy youth,
Renown'd alike for gallantry and truth.

St. James's bell had toll'd some wretches in,
(As tatter'd riding-hoods alone could sin)
The happier sinners now their charms recruit,
And to their manteaus their complexion suit;
The opera queens had finish'd half their faces,
And city dames already taken places;
Fops of all kinds, to see the Lion, run;
The beauties stay till the first act's begun,
And beaux step home to put fresh linen on.

Lord Viscount Hervey.

No well-dress'd youth in coffee-house remain'd
But pensive Patch, who on the window lean'd;
And Silliander, that alert, and gay,
First pick'd his teeth, and then began to say.

SILLIANDER.

Why all these sighs; ah! why so pensive grown?
Some cause there is why thus you sit alone.
Does hapless passion all this sorrow move?
Or dost thou envy where the ladies love?

PATCH.

If, whom they love, my envy must pursue,
'Tis true, at least, I never envy you.

SILLIANDER.

No, I'm unhappy—you are in the right—
'Tis you they favour, and 'tis me they slight.
Yet I could tell, but that I hate to boast,
A club of ladies where 'tis me they toast.

PATCH.

Toasting does seldom any favour prove;
Like us, they never toast the thing they love.
A certain duke one night my health begun;
With chearful pledges round the room it run,
'Till the young Silvia, press'd to drink it too,
Started and vow'd she knew not what to do:
What, drink a fellow's health! she dy'd with shame:
Yet blush'd whenever she pronounc'd my name.

SILLIANDER.

Ill fates pursue me, may I never find
The dice propitious, or the ladies kind,
If fair Miss Flippy's fan I did not tear,
And one from me she condescends to wear.

PATCH.

Women are always ready to receive;
'Tis then a favour when the sex will give.
A lady (but she is too great to name)
Beauteous in person, spotless in her fame,

With gentle strugglings let me force this ring;
Another day may give another thing.

SILLIANDER.

I could say something—see this billet-doux—
And as for presents—look upon my shoe—
These buckles were not forc'd, nor half a theft,
But a young countess fondly made the gift.

PATCH.

My countess is more nice, more artful too,
Affects to fly, that I may fierce pursue:
This snuff-box which I begg'd, she still deny'd,
And when I strove to snatch it, seem'd to hide;
She laugh'd and fled, and as I sought to seize,
With affectation cram'd it down her stays;
Yet hop'd she did not place it there unseen,
I press'd her breasts, and pull'd it from between.

SILLIANDER.

Last night, as I stood ogling of her grace,
Drinking delicious poison from her face,

The soft enchantress did that face decline,
Nor ever rais'd her eyes to meet with mine;
With sudden art some secret did pretend,
Lean'd cross two chairs to whisper to a friend,
While the stiff whalebone with the motion rose,
And thousand beauties to my sight expose.

PATCH.

Early this morn—(but I was ask'd to come)
I drank bohea in Celia's dressing-room:
Warm from her bed, to me alone within,
Her night-gown fasten'd with a single pin;
Her night-cloaths tumbled with resistless grace,
And her bright hair play'd careless round her face;
Reaching the kettle made her gown unpin,
She wore no waistcoat, and her shift was thin.

SILLIANDER.

See Titiana driving to the park!
Haste! let us follow 'tis not yet too dark:
In her all beauties of the spring are seen,
Her cheeks are rosy, and her mantle green.

PATCH.

See Tintoretta to the opera goes!
Haste, or the crowd will not permit our bows;
In her the glory of the heav'ns we view,
Her eyes are star-like, and her mantle blue.

SILLIANDER.

What colour does in Celia's stockings shine?
Reveal that secret, and the prize is thine.

PATCH.

What are her garters? tell me if you can;
I'll freely own thee far the happier man.

Thus Patch continued his heroic strain,
While Silliander but contends in vain,
After a conquest so important gain'd,
Unrival'd Patch in every ruelle reign'd.

WEDNESDAY.

THE TETE-A-TETE.

DANCINDA.

"NO, fair Dancinda, no; you strive in vain
To calm my care, and mitigate my pain;
If all my sighs, my cares, can fail to move,
Ah! soothe me not with fruitless vows of love."
Thus Strephon spoke. Dancinda thus reply'd:
"What must I do to gratify your pride?
Too well you know (ungrateful as thou art)
How much you triumph in this tender heart:
What proof of love remains for me to grant?
Yet still you teaze me with some new complaint.
Oh! would to Heaven!—but the fond wish is vain—
Too many favours had not made it plain!
But such a passion breaks through all disguise,
Love reddens on my cheek, and wishes in my eyes.
Is't not enough (inhuman and unkind!)
I own the secret conflict of my mind;
You cannot know what secret pain I prove,
When I, with burning blushes, own I love.

You see my artless joy at your approach,
I sigh, I faint, I tremble at your touch;
And in your absence all the world I shun;
I hate mankind, and curse the cheering sun.
Still as I fly, ten thousand swains pursue;
Ten thousand swains I sacrifice to you.
I shew you all my heart without disguise:
But these are tender proofs that you despise—
I see too well what wishes you pursue;
You would not only conquer, but undo:
You, cruel victor, weary of your flame,
Would seek a cure in my eternal shame;
And, not content my honour to subdue,
Now strive to triumph o'er my virtue too.
Oh! Love, a God indeed to womankind,
Whose arrows burn me, and whose fetters bind,
Avenge thy altars, vindicate thy fame,
And blast these traitors that profane thy name;
Who, by pretending to thy sacred fire,
Raise cursed trophies to impure desire.

"Have you forgot with what ensnaring art
You first seduc'd this fond uncautious heart?

Then as I fled, did you not kneeling cry,
'Turn, cruel beauty; whither would you fly?
Why all these doubts? why this distrustful fear?
No impious wishes shall offend your ear:
Nor ever shall my boldest hopes pretend
Above the title of a tender friend;
Blest, if my lovely goddess will permit
My humble vows thus sighing at her feet.
The tyrant, Love, that in my bosom reigns,
The God himself submits to wear your chains:
You shall direct his course, his ardor tame,
And check the fury of his wildest flame.'

"Unpractis'd youth is easily deceiv'd;
Sooth'd by such sounds, I listen'd and believ'd:
Now quite forgot that soft submissive fear,
You dare to ask what I must blush to hear.

"Could I forget the honour of my race,
And meet your wishes, fearless of disgrace;
Could passion o'er my tender youth prevail,
And all my mother's pious maxims fail;

Yet to preserve your heart (which still must be,
False as it is, for ever dear to me)
This fatal proof of love I would not give,
Which you'd contemn the moment you receive.
The wretched she, who yields to guilty joys,
A man may pity, but he must despise.
Your ardour ceas'd, I then should see you shun
The wretched victim by your arts undone.
Yet if I could that cold indifference bear,
What more would strike me with the last despair,
With this reflection would my soul be torn,
To know I merited your cruel scorn.

"Has love no pleasures free from guilt or fear?
Pleasures less fierce, more lasting, more sincere?
Thus let us gently kiss and fondly gaze,
Love is a child, and like a child he plays.

"O, Strephon, if you would continue just,
If love be something more than brutal lust,
Forbear to ask what I must still deny,
This bitter pleasure, this destructive joy,

So closely followed by the dismal train
Of cutting shame, and guilt's heart-piercing pain."

She paus'd, and fix'd her eyes upon her fan;
He took a pinch of snuff, and thus began:
"Madam, if love—" but he could say no more,
For Mademoiselle came rapping at the door.
The dangerous moments no adieus afford;
—"Begone, she cries, I'm sure I hear my lord."
The lover starts from his unfinish'd loves,
To snatch his hat, and seek his scatter'd gloves:
The sighing dame to meet her dear prepares,
While Strephon, cursing, slips down the back-
stairs.

THURSDAY.

THE BASSETTE TABLE.

SMILINDA AND CARDELIA.

CARDELIA.

THE *Bassette-table* spread, the Tallier come;
Why stays Smilinda in her dressing-room?
Rise, pensive nymph! the Tallier waits for you:

SMILINDA.

Ah! madam, since my Sharper is untrue,
I joyless make my once ador'd *alpiu*.
I saw him stand behind Ombrelia's chair,
And whisper with that soft deluding air,
And those feign'd sighs, which cheat the list'ning fair.

CARDELIA.

Is this the cause of your romantic strains?
A mightier grief my heavier heart sustains.

As you by Love, so I by Fortune cross'd;
In one bad *deal* three *septlevas* have lost.

SMILINDA.

Is that the grief which you compare with mine?
With ease the smiles of Fortune I resign:
Would all my gold in one bad *deal* were gone;
Were lovely Sharper mine, and mine alone.

CARDELIA.

A lover lost is but a common care;
And prudent nymphs against that change prepare.
The knave of clubs thrice lost: oh! who could guess
This fatal stroke! this unforeseen distress?

SMILINDA.

See! Betty Loveit very *a-propos*,
She all the care of *love* and *play* does know;
Dear Betty shall th' important point decide;
Betty, who oft the pain of each has try'd;
Impartial she shall say who suffers most,
By *cards' ill usage*, or by *lovers lost*

LOVEIT.

Tell, tell your griefs; attentive will I stay,
Though time is precious, and I want some tea.

CARDELIA.

Behold this *equipage*, by Mathers wrought,
With fifty guineas (a great pen'orth!) bought.
See on the tooth-pick, Mars and Cupid strive;
And both the struggling figures seem alive.
Upon the bottom shines the queen's bright face;
A myrtle foliage round the thimble case.
Jove, Jove himself, does on the scissars shine;
The metal, and the workmanship divine!

SMILINDA.

This *snuff-box*, once the pledge of Sharper's love,
When rival beauties for the present strove;
At Corticelli's he the raffle won;
Then first his passion was in public shown:
Hazardia blush'd, and turned her head aside,
A rival's envy (all in vain) to hide.
This *snuff-box*—on the hinge see brilli ants shine—
This *snuff-box* will I stake; the prize is mine.

CARDELIA.

Alas! far lesser losses than I bear
Have made a soldier sigh, a lover swear.
And oh! what makes the disappointment hard,
'Twas my own lord that drew the fatal card.
In complaisance I took the *queen* he gave;
Though my own secret wish was for the knave:
The *knave* won Sonica which I had chose;
And the next *pull* my *septleva* I lose.

SMILINDA.

But ah! what aggravates the killing smart,
The cruel thought that stabs me to the heart;
This curs'd Ombrelia, this undoing fair,
By whose vile arts this heavy grief I bear;
She, at whose name I shed these spiteful tears,
She owes to me the very charms she wears:
An awkward thing when first she came to town;
Her shape unfashion'd, and her face unknown:
She was my friend, I taught her first to spread
Upon her sallow cheeks enlivening red.

I introduc'd her to the Park and plays;
And by my int'rest Cosins made her stays.
Ungrateful wretch! with mimic airs grown pert,
She dares to steal my favourite lover's heart.

CARDELIA.

Wretch that I was! how often have I swore,
When Winnall tallied, I would *punt* no more?
I know the bite, yet to my ruin run;
And see the folly which I cannot shun.

SMILINDA.

How many maids have Sharper's vows deceiv'd?
How many curs'd the moment they believ'd?
Yet his known falshoods could no warning prove:
Ah! what is warning to a maid in love?

CARDELIA.

But of what marble must that breast be form'd,
To gaze on Bassette, and remain unwarm'd?
When *kings*, *queens*, *knaves*, are set in decent rank,
Expos'd in glorious heaps the tempting bank,

Guineas, half-guineas, all the shining train;
The winner's pleasure, and the loser's pain:
In bright confusion open *rouleaus* lie,
They strike the soul, and glitter in the eye,
Fir'd by the sight, all reason I disdain;
My passions rise, and will not bear the rein.
Look upon Bassette, you who reason boast;
And see if reason must not *there* be lost.

SMILINDA.

What more than marble must that heart compose,
Can hearken coldly to my Sharper's vows?
Then when he trembles, when his blushes rise,
When awful love seems melting in his eyes,
With eager beats his Mechlin cravat moves:
He loves, I whisper to myself, *he loves!*
Such unfeign'd passion in his looks appears,
I lose all mem'ry of my former fears:
My panting heart confesses all his charms,
I yield at once, and sink into his arms:

Think of that moment; you who prudence boast;
For such a moment, prudence well were lost.

CARDELIA.

At the *Groom-porter's*, batter'd bullies play,
Some *dukes* at Marybone bowl time away.
But who the bowl, or rattling dice compares
To Bassette's heavenly joys, and pleasing care?

SMILINDA.

Soft Simplicetta doats upon a beau;
Prudina likes a man, and laughs at show.
Their several graces in my Sharper meet;
Strong as the footman, as the master sweet.

LOVEIT.

Cease your contention, which has been too long;
I grow impatient, and the tea too strong.
Attend, and yield to what I now decide;
The *equipage* shall grace Smilinda's side:
The snuff-box to Cardelia I decree,
Now leave complaining, and begin your *tea*

FRIDAY.

THE TOILETTE.

LYDIA.

NOW twenty springs had cloath'd the Park
with green,
Since Lydia knew the blossom of fifteen;
No lovers now her morning hours molest;
And catch her at her toilette half undrest.
The thund'ring knocker wakes the street no more,
Nor chairs, nor coaches, croud the silent door;
Now at the window all her mornings pass,
Or at the dumb devotion of her glass:
Reclin'd upon her arm she pensive sate,
And curs'd th' inconstancy of man too late.

"Oh youth! O spring of life, for ever lost!
No more my name shall reign the fav'rite toast:
On glass no more the diamond grave my name,
And lines mis-spelt record my lover's flame:
Nor shall side-boxes watch my wand'ring eyes,
And, as they catch the glance, in rows arise

With humble bows; nor white-glov'd beaus encroach
In crouds behind, to guard me to my coach.

"What shall I do to spend the hateful day?
At chapel shall I wear the morn away?
Who there appears at these unmodish hours,
But ancient matrons with their frizzled tow'rs,
And grey religious maids? my presence there
Amidst that sober train, would own despair;
Nor am I yet so old, nor is my glance
As yet fix'd wholly on devotion's trance.
Strait then I'll dress, and take my wonted range
Through India shops, to Motteux's, or the Change,
Where the tall jar erects its stately pride,
With antic shapes in China's azure dy'd;
There careless lies a rich brocade unroll'd,
Here shines a cabinet with burnish'd gold.
But then, alas! I must be forc'd to pay,
And bring no penn'orths, not a fan away!

"How am I curs'd, unhappy and forlorn!
My lover's triumph, and my sex's scorn!

False is the pompous grief of youthful heirs;
False are the loose coquet's inveigling airs;
False is the crafty courtier's plighted word;
False are the dice when gamesters stamp the board;
False is the sprightly widow's public tear;
Yet these to Damon's oaths are all sincere.

"For what young flirt, base man, am I abus'd?
To please your wife am I unkindly us'd?
'Tis true her face may boast the peach's bloom;
But does her nearer whisper breathe perfume?
I own her taper shape is form'd to please;
But don't you see her unconfin'd by stays?
She doubly to fifteen may claim pretence;
Alike we read it in her face and sense.
Insipid, servile thing? whom I disdain!
Her phlegm can best support the marriage chain.
Damon is practis'd in the modish life;
Can hate, and yet be civil to his wife;
He games, he drinks, he swears, he fights, he roves;
Yet Cloe can believe he fondly loves.

Mistress and wife by turns supply his need;
A miss for pleasure, and a wife for breed.
Powder'd with diamonds, free from spleen or care,
She can a sullen husband's humour bear;
Her cred'lous friendship, and her stupid ease,
Have often been my jest in happier days;
Now Cloe boasts and triumphs in my pains;
To her he's faithful; 'tis to me he feigns.
Am I that stupid thing to bear neglect,
And force a smile, not daring to suspect?
No perjur'd man! a wife may be content,
But you shall find a mistress can resent."

Thus love-sick Lydia rav'd; her maid appears,
And in her faithful hand the band-box bears;
(The Cestus that reform'd inconstant Jove
Not better fill'd with what allur'd to love)
"How well this ribband's gloss becomes your face!"
She cries in rapture; "then so sweet a lace!
How charmingly you look! so bright! so fair!
'Tis to your eyes the head-dress owes its air!"
Strait Lydia smil'd; the comb adjusts her locks;
And at the play-house, Harry keeps her box.

SATURDAY.

THE SMALL POX.

FLAVIA.

THE wretched Flavia on her couch reclin'd,
Thus breath'd the anguish of a wounded mind,
A glass revers'd in her right hand she bore,
For now she shun'd the face she sought before.

"How am I chang'd! alas! how am I grown
A frightful spectre, to myself unknown!
Where's my complexion? where my radiant bloom,
That promis'd happiness for years to come?
Then with what pleasure I this face survey'd!
To look once more, my visits oft delay'd!
Charm'd with the view, a fresher red would rise,
And a new life shot sparkling from my eyes!

"Ah! faithless glass, my wonted bloom restore;
Alas! I rave, that bloom is now no more!
The greatest good the gods on men bestow,
E'en youth itself to me is useless now.

There was a time (oh! that I could forget!)
When opera-tickets pour'd before my feet;
And at the ring, where brightest beauties shine,
The earliest cherries of the spring were mine.
Witness, O Lilly; and thou, Motteux, tell,
How much japan these eyes have made ye sell.
With what contempt ye saw me oft despise
The humble offer of the raffled prize;
For at each raffle still each prize I bore,
With scorn rejected, or with triumph wore!
Now beauty's fled, and presents are no more!

"For me the Patriot has the house forsook,
And left debates to catch a passing look:
For me the Soldier has soft verses writ:
For me the Beau has aim'd to be a wit.
For me the Wit to nonsense was betray'd;
The Gamester has for me his dun delay'd,
And overseen the card he would have play'd.
The bold and haughty by success made vain,
Aw'd by my eyes, have trembled to complain:

The bashful 'Squire touch'd by a wish unknown,
Has dar'd to speak with spirit not his own:
Fir'd by one wish, all did alike adore;
Now beauty's fled, and lovers are no more!

"As round the room I turn my weeping eyes,
New unaffected scenes of sorrow rise.
Far from my sight that killing picture bear,
The face disfigure, and the canvass tear:
That picture which with pride I us'd to show,
The lost resemblance but upbraids me now.
And thou, my toilette! where I oft have sate,
While hours unheeded pass'd in deep debate,
How curls should fall, or where a patch to place;
If blue or scarlet best became my face:
Now on some happier nymph your aid bestow;
On fairer heads, ye useless jewels glow!
No borrowed lustre can my charms restore;
Beauty is fled, and dress is now no more!

"Ye meaner beauties, I permit ye shine;
Go, triumph in the hearts that once were mine:

But 'midst your triumphs with confusion know,
'Tis to my ruin all your arms ye owe.
Would pitying Heav'n restore my wonted mien,
Ye still might move unthought of and unseen:
But oh, how vain, how wretched is the boast
Of beauty faded, and of empire lost!
What now is left but weeping, to deplore
My beauty fled, and empire now no more?

"Ye cruel chemists, what withheld your aid!
Could no pomatum save a trembling maid?
How false and trifling is that art ye boast!
No art can give me back my beauty lost.
In tears surrounded by my friends I lay
Mask'd o'er, and trembled at the sight of day;
Mirmillio came my fortune to deplore,
(A golden-headed cane well carv'd he bore)
Cordials, he cry'd, my spirits must restore!
Beauty is fled, and spirit is no more!

"Galen, the grave, officious Squirt, was there,
With fruitless grief and unavailing care;

Machaon too, the great Machaon, known
By his red cloak and his superior frown;
And why, he cry'd, this grief and this despair,
You shall again be well, again be fair;
Believe my oath; (with that an oath he swore)
False was his oath; my beauty was no more!

"Cease, hapless maid, no more thy tale pursue.
Forsake mankind, and bid the world adieu!
Monarchs and beauties rule with equal sway;
All strive to serve, and glory to obey:
Alike unpitied when depos'd they grow,
Men mock the idol of their former vow.

"Adieu! ye parks!—in some obscure recess,
Where gentle streams will weep at my distress,
Where no false friend will in my grief take part,
And mourn my ruin with a joyful heart;
There let me live in some deserted place,
There hide in shades this lost inglorious face.
Plays, operas, circles, I no more must view!
My toilette, patches, all the world adieu!"

VERSES,

WRITTEN IN THE CHIOSK OF THE BRITISH-PALACE, AT PERA, OVERLOOKING THE CITY OF CONSTANTINOPLE, DECEMBER 26, 1718.

GIVE me, great God! ſaid I, a little farm,
In summer shady, and in winter warm;
Where a clear spring gives birth to murm'ring brooks,
By nature gliding down the mossy rocks.
Not artfully by leaden pipes convey'd,
Or greatly falling in a forc'd cascade,
Pure and unsully'd winding thro' the shade.
All-bounteous Heaven has added to my prayer
A softer climate, and a purer air.

Our frozen Isle now chilling winter binds,
Deform'd by rains, and rough with blasting winds;
The wither'd woods grow white with hoary frost,
By driving storms their verdant beauty lost;
The trembling birds their leafless covert shun,
And seek in distant climes a warmer sun:

all the verses & Prose in this Book
were wrote by me, without ye assistance
of one line from any other.

Mary Wortley Montagu

The water-nymphs their silent urns deplore,
E'en Thames benumb'd 's a river now no more:
The barren meads no longer yield delight,
By glist'ring snows made painful to the sight.

Here summer reigns with one eternal smile,
Succeeding harvests bless the happy soil.
Fair fertile fields, to whom indulgent Heaven
Has ev'ry charm of ev'ry season given;
No killing cold deforms the beauteous year,
The springing flowers no coming winter fear.
But as the parent Rose decays and dies,
The infant buds with brighter colours rise,
And with fresh sweets the mother's scent supplies.
Near them the Violet grows with odours blest,
And blooms in more than Tyrian purple drest;
The rich Jonquils their golden beams display,
And shine in glory's emulating day;
The peaceful groves their verdant leaves retain,
The streams still murmur, undefil'd with rain,
And tow'ring greens adorn the fruitful plain

The warbling kind uninterrupted sing,
Warm'd with enjoyments of perpetual spring.

Here, at my window, I at once survey
The crowded city and resounding sea;
In distant views the Asian mountains rise,
And lose their snowy summits in the skies;
Above these mountains proud Olympus tow'rs,
The parliamental seat of heavenly powers,
New to the sight, my ravish'd eyes admire
Each gilded crescent and each antique spire,
The marble mosques, beneath whose ample domes
Fierce warlike sultans sleep in peaceful tombs;
Those lofty structures, once the Christians' boast,
Their names, their beauty, and their honours lost;
Those altars bright with gold and sculpture grac'd,
By barb'rous zeal of savage foes defac'd;
Soph'a alone, her ancient name retains,
Tho' unbelieving vows her shrine profanes;
Where holy saints have died in sacred cells,
Where monarchs pray'd the frantic Dervise dwells,

How art thou fall'n, imperial city, low!
Where are thy hopes of Roman glory now?
Where are thy palaces by prelates rais'd?
Where Grecian artists all their skill display'd,
Before the happy sciences decay'd;
So vast, that youthful kings might here reside,
So splendid, to content a patriarch's pride;
Convents where emperors profess'd of old,
The labour'd pillars that their triumphs told;
Vain monuments of them that once were great,
Sunk undistinguish'd by one common fate;
One little spot the tenure small contains,
Of Greek nobility the poor remains.
Where other Helens, with like powerful charms,
Had once engag'd the warring world in arms;
Those names which royal ancestors can boast,
In mean mechanic arts obscurely lost;
Those eyes a second Homer might inspire,
Fix'd at the loom, destroy their useless fire;
Griev'd at a view which struck upon my mind
The short-liv'd vanity of human kind.

In gaudy objects I indulge my sight,
And turn where Eastern pomp gives gay delight;
See the vast train in various habits drest
By the bright scimitar and sable vest,
The proud vizier distinguish'd o'er the rest;
Six slaves in gay attire his bridle hold,
His bridle rich with gems, and stirrups gold;
His snowy steed adorn'd with costly pride,
Whole troops of soldiers mounted by his side,
These top the plumy crest Arabian courtiers guide.
With artful duty all decline their eyes,
No bellowing shouts of noisy crowds arise;
Silence, in solemn state, the march attends,
Till at the dread divan the slow procession ends.

Yet not these prospects all profusely gay,
The gilded navy that adorns the sea,
The rising city in confusion fair,
Magnificently form'd, irregular,
Where woods and palaces at once surprise,
Gardens on gardens, domes on domes arise,
And endless beauties tire the wand'ring eyes,

So sooth my wishes, or so charm my mind,
As this retreat secure from human kind.
No knave's successful craft does spleen excite,
No coxcomb's tawdry splendor shocks my sight;
No mob-alarm awakes my female fear,
No praise my mind, nor envy hurts my ear,
E'en fame itself can hardly reach me here;
Impertinence with all her tattling train,
Fair-sounding flattery's delicious bane;
Censorious folly, noisy party-rage,
The thousand tongues with which she must engage;
Who dares have virtue in a vicious age.

EPILOGUE*

TO MARY, QUEEN OF SCOTS.

DESIGNED TO BE SPOKEN BY MRS. OLDFIELD.

WHAT could luxurious woman wish for more,
To fix her joys, or to extend her pow'r?
Their every wish was in this Mary seen,
Gay, witty, youthful, beauteous, and a queen.
Vain useless blessings with ill-conduct join'd!
Light as the air, and fleeting as the wind.
Whatever poets write, and lovers vow,
Beauty, what poor omnipotence hast thou!

Queen Bess had wisdom, council, power, and laws;
How few espous'd a wretched beauty's cause!

* This Epilogue was intended for a Play on the Story of Mary Queen of Scots, which Philip Duke of Wharton began to write, but never finished. No part of the Play now remains, but these four lines:

Sure were I free, and Norfolk were a prisoner,
I'd fly with more impatience to his arms,
Than the poor Israelite gaz'd on the serpent,
When life was the reward of every look.

Walpole's Catalogue, vol. II. p. 134.

Learn thence, ye fair, more solid charms to prize;
Contemn the idle flatt'rers of your eyes.
The brightest object shines but while 'tis new:
That influence lessens by familiar view.
Monarchs and beauties rule with equal sway,
All strive to serve, and glory to obey;
Alike unpitied when depos'd they grow——
Men mock the idol of their former vow.

Two great examples have been shewn to-day,
To what sure ruin passion does betray;
What long repentance to short joys is due;
When reason rules, what glory must ensue.

If you will love, love like Eliza then;
Love for amusement, like those traitors, men.
Think that the pastime of a leisure hour
She favour'd oft—but never shar'd her pow'r.

The traveller by desart wolves pursu'd,
If by his art the savage foe's subdu'd,

The world will still the noble act applaud,
Tho' victory was gain'd by needful fraud.

Such is, my tender sex, our helpless case;
And such the barbarous heart, hid by the begging face
By passion fir'd, and not withheld by shame,
They cruel hunters are, we trembling game.
Trust me, dear ladies, (for I know 'em well)
They burn to triumph, and they sigh to tell:
Cruel to them that yield, cullies to them that sell.
Believe me, 'tis by far the wiser course,
Superior art should meet superior force:
Hear, but be faithful to your int'rest still:
Secure your hearts—then fool with whom you will.

EPILOGUE

TO THE TRAGEDY OF CATO.

YOU see in ancient Rome what folly reign'd;
A folly British men would have disdain'd.
Here's none so weak to pity Cato's case,
Who might have liv'd, and had a handsome place;
But rashly vain, and insolently great,
He perish'd by his fault and not his fate.
Thank Heav'n! our patriots better ends pursue,
With something more than glory in their view.
Poets write morals—priests for martyrs preach—
Neither such fools to practise what they teach.

Tho' your dear country much you wish to serve,
For bonny Britons 'tis too hard to starve;
Or what's all one, to any generous mind,
From girls, Champagne, and gaming, be confin'd;
Portius might well obey his sire's command,
Returning to his small paternal land;
A low estate was ample to support
His private life, far distant from the court;

Far from the crowd of emulating beaux,
Where Martia never wanted birth-day clothes.

For you, who live in these more polish'd days,
To spend your money, lo! ten thousand ways;
Dice may run ill, or duns demand their due,
And ways to get (God knows) are very few;
In times so differing, who shall harshly blame
Our modern heroes, not to act the same.

TO A FRIEND

ON HIS TRAVELS.

FROM this vile town immers'd in smoke and
care,
To you who brighten in a purer air,
Your faithful friend conveys her tenderest thought,
(Tho' now perhaps neglected and forgot)
May blooming health your wonted mirth restore,
And every pleasure crown your every hour;
Cares'd, esteem'd, and lov'd, your merit known,
And foreign lands admire you, like your own:
Whilst I in silence various fortunes bear,
Distracted with the rage of bosom-war;
My restless fever tears my changeful brain,
With mix'd ideas of delight and pain;
Sometimes soft views my morning dreams employ
In the faint dawn of visionary joy:
Which rigid reason quickly drives away,
I seek the shade and fly from rising day;
In pleasing madness meet some moments ease,
And fondly cherish my belov'd disease.

If female weakness melt my woman's mind
At least no weakness in the choice I find;
Not soothed to softness by a warbling flute,
Nor the bought merit of a birth-day suit;
Not lost my heart by the surprising skill
In opera tunes, in dancing, or quadrille.
The only charm my inclination moves
Is such a virtue, Heaven itself approves!
A soul superior to each vulgar view,
Great, steady, gentle, generous, and true.
How I regret my trifling hours past,
And look with sorrow o'er the dreary waste!
In false pursuits and vanity bestow'd
The perfect image of a dirty road;
Through puddles oft, o'er craggy rocks I stray,
A tiresome dull uncomfortable way:
And after toiling long through thick and thin
To reach some meanly mercenary inn.
The bills are high, and very bad the fare,
I curse the wretched entertainment there:
And jogging on, resolve to stop no more
Where gaudy signs invite me to the door.

TO THE SAME.

THOUGH old in ill the traitor sure shall find
Some secret sting transfix his guilty mind.
Though bribes or favour may protect his fame,
Or fear restrain invectives on his name;
None 'quits himself—his own impartial thought
Condemns—and conscience shall record the fault.
Yet more, my friend! your happy state may bear
This disappointment as below your care.
For what you have return to Heav'n your thanks,
Few share the prizes, many draw the blanks.
Of breach of promise oudly you complain,
Have you then known the world so long in vain?
Worse than the iron age, our impious times
Have learn'd to laugh at most flagitious crimes.
Are you to know that 'tis a jest to find
Unthinking honesty pervade the mind?
At best, they say, the man is strangely odd
Who keeps his oath, and can believe a God.
This was the cant, when Edward held the throne,
Before Sp:nosa wrote, or Hobbes was known;

When the gilt Bible was the king's delight,
When prayer preceded day, and hymns the night.
Now softening eunuchs sing Italian airs,
The dancing dame to midnight ball repairs.

Now, if an honest man (like you) I view,
Contemning interest, and to virtue true,
I deem, he deviates from nature's rules,
Like burning hills, or petrifying pools.
I stand astonish'd at the strange portent,
And think some revolution the event;
As all grave heads were startled as they heard
That a new comet in the west appear'd;
When, from a human mother* rabbits sprung,
And Ward his pills like hand granadoes flung;
When *gratis* scattering cures amidst the crowd—
A miracle! as Charteris† swears aloud—
A greater miracle I daily see
The ancient faith of Pius reign in thee.

* Mary Tofts, the rabbit-woman of Godalmin.

† Colonel Charteris, of infamous memory, satirised by Pope and Arbuthnot.

Observe the wretch, who has that faith forsook,
How clear his voice, and how assured his look!
Like innocence, and as serenely bold,
Conscious protection of almighty gold!
Whilst thus he reasons to relieve his fears:
"Oft I've deceiv'd, yet still have kept my ears,
I have been threat'ned for a broken vow,
And yet successfully have laugh'd till now,
And will laugh on, my fortune's not the worse,
When starving cullies rail, or vainly curse."
Shall then the villain 'scape? such knaves as he
Be rich and safe, and from all vengeance free?
Consider friend! but coolly, and you'll find,
Revenge the frailty of a feeble mind;
Nor think he 'scapes tho' he should never feel
The pangs of poison, or the force of steel.
There is a time when conscience shakes the soul,
When Toland's tenets cannot fear controul,
When secret anguish fills the anxious breast,
Vacant from business, nor compos'd by rest;
Then dreams invade, the injured Gods appear
All armed with thunder and awake his fear;

The wretch will start at every flash that flies,
Grow pale at the first murmur of the skies;
Then, if a fever fires corrupted blood,
In every fit he feels the hand of God.
Trembling and sunk into the last despair,
He dares not offer one repenting prayer;
For how can hope with desperate guilt agree,
And the worst beast is worthier life than he;
This, at the best will be his certain fate,
Or Heav'n may sooner think his crimes complete.

FRAGMENT TO

* * * * * * * * * * *

LET mules and asses in that circle tread,
And proud of trappings toss a feather'd head;
Leave you the stupid business of the state,
Strive to be happy, and despise the great:
Come where the Graces guide the gentle day,
Where Venus rules amidst her native sea,
Where at her altar gallantries appear,
And even Wisdom dares not shew severe.

* * * * * * * * * * * * * * *

* * * * * * * * * * * * * * *

TO Mr.————

FOR ever blest be that prolific brain
Which can such store of images contain!
Thus the charged trees, with blooming odours crown'd,
Shed their fair blossoms with profusion round.
So swells the brook with heav'n descended rain
And flows meand'ring on the thirsty plain;
Such various tälents were by Heaven design'd,
(Too vast a treasure for a single mind).
To please, astonish, and instruct mankind
With a delight, not to be told, I view
Themes long exhausted in your hands grow new;
Past all describing your descriptions are,
So full, so just, so bold, yet regular;
The style so varied that it wants a name,
Which ever differing, ever is the same;
You raise or calm our passions as you please,
The human heart your powerful pen obeys.
When eager Trasimond pursues the course,
We hear the whip and see the foaming horse;

With soft Sophronia we have wept and smil'd,
So soon offended—sooner reconcil'd.

Go on great Author! that the world may see
How bright, when from pedantic fetters free;
True genius shines, and shines alone in thee.
Give new editions, with a noble scorn
Of insect critics, who'd obscure thy morn;
Neglect their censures, nor thy work delay,
The owls still sicken at the sight of day.

JOHN DUKE OF MARLBOROUGH.

WHEN the proud Frenchman's strong rapacious hand
Spread over Europe ruin and command,
Our sinking temples and expiring law
With trembling dread the rolling tempest saw;
Destined a province to insulting Gaul,
This Genius rose, and stopp'd the ponderous fall.
His temperate valour form'd no giddy scheme,
No victory rais'd him to a rage of fame;
The happy temper of his even mind
No danger e'er could shock, or conquest blind.
Fashion'd alike, by Nature and by Art,
To please, engage, and interest, every heart.
In public life by all who saw approv'd,
In private hours by all who knew him lov'd.

A CHARACTER.

THO' a strong vanity may you persuade
You are not for a politician made;
Your tropes are drawn from Robin Walpole's
head,
Your sense is but repeating what he said;
An useful puppy, eminently known,
As proud to father what he will not own.
Some arguments he leaves you to expose,
So valets flutter in my lord's old clothes.
But, should he strip you of his borrow'd sense,
How poorly thin your boasted eloquence!
Know your own talents better, I advise;
Be brisk, yet dull, but aim not to look wise:
In low insipid rhimes place your delight,
Laugh without jests, and without reading write.
Despis'd by men, in ladies' ruels sit,
Where country coquettes bolster up your wit.
May all your minuets applauses meet!
An able coxcomb only in your feet.

By fawning lies, in leagues with court-knaves
grow,
And smile on beauties, whom you *do not know.*
Then, acting all the coyness of a lover,
Your *no-intrigue* endeavour to discover.
Aiming at wit, in many an evil hour,
Have the perpetual will without the power.
Conceit for *breeding*, rude for easy take,
Horseplay for wit, and noise for mirth mistake.
Love's perfect joys to perfect men belong;
Seek you but *the occasion for a song.*
Thus to the end of life may you remain
A merry blockhead, treacherous and vain.

AN ANSWER TO A LOVE LETTER,

IN VERSE.

IS it to me this sad lamenting strain?
Are Heaven's choicest gifts bestow'd in vain?
A plenteous fortune and a beauteous bride,
Your love rewarded, and content your pride;
Yet, leaving her, 'tis me that you pursue,
Without one single charm—but being new.
How vile is man! how I detest the ways
Of covert falsehood, and designing praise!
As tasteless, easier happiness you slight,
Ruin your joy, and mischief your delight.
Why should poor Pug (the mimic of your kind)
Wear a rough chain, and be to box confin'd?
Some cup, perhaps, he breaks, or tears a fan,
While moves, unpunish'd, the destroyer man,
Not bound by vows, and unrestrain'd by shame,
In sport you break the heart, and rend the fame.
Not that your art can be successful here,
Th' already plunder'd need no robber fear

Nor sighs, nor charms, nor flattery, can move,
Too well secur'd against a second love.
Once, and but once, that devil charm'd my mind,
To reason deaf, to observation blind,
I idly hop'd, (what cannot Love persuade)
My fondness equal'd, and my truth repaid:
Slow to distrust, and willing to believe;
Long hush'd my doubts, I would myself deceive.
But oh! too soon—this tale would ever last—
Sleep on my wrongs, and let me think them past.
For you, who mourn with counterfeited grief,
And ask so boldly, like a begging thief,
May soon some other nymph inflict the pain,
You know so well with cruel art to feign.
Tho' long you've sported with Don Cupid's dart,
You *may* see eyes, and you *may* feel a heart.
So the brisk wits who stop the evening-coach,
Laugh at the fear that follows their approach;
With idle mirth and haughty scorn despise
The passenger's pale cheek, and staring eyes;
But, seiz'd by Justice, find a fright no jest,
And all the terror doubl'd in their breast.

LORD HERVEY TO MR. FOX.

WRITTEN AT FLORENCE, 1729, IN IMITATION OF THE SIXTH ODE OF THE SECOND BOOK OF HORACE.

" Septimi Gades aditure mecum."

THOU, dearest youth, who taught me first to know
What pleasures from a real friendship flow ;
Where neither interest nor deceit have part,
But all the warmth is native of the heart.
Thou know'st to comfort, soothe, or entertain,
Joy of my health, and cordial to my pain ;
When life seem'd failing in her latest stage,
And fell disease anticipated age ;
When wasting sickness, and afflictive pain,
By Æsculapius' sons oppos'd in vain,
Forc'd me reluctant, desperate to explore
A warmer sun, and seek a milder shore,
Thy steady love, with unexampled truth,
Forsook each gay companion of thy youth,
Whate'er the prosperous, or the great employs,
Business and interest, and love's softer joys.

The weary steps of misery to attend,
To share distress, and make a wretch thy friend.
If o'er the mountain's snowy top we stray,
Where Carthage first explor'd the vent'rous way;
Or thro' the tainted air of Rome's parch'd plains,
Where want resides and superstition reigns,
Cheerful and unrepining still you bear
Each dangerous rigour of the varying year;
And kindly anxious for thy friend alone,
Lament his sufferings, and forget thy own.
Oh! would kind Heaven, those tedious sufferings
past,
Permit me, Ickworth, rest and health at last!
In that lov'd shade, my youth's delightful seat,
My early pleasures, and my late retreat,
Where lavish Nature's favourite blessings flow,
And all the seasons all their sweets bestow.
There might I trifle carelessly away
The milder evening of life's clouded day;
From business and the world's intrusion free,
With books, with love, with beauty, and with
thee.

No farther want, no wish, yet unpossess'd,
Could e'er disturb this unambitious breast.
Let those who Fortune's shining gifts implore,
Who sue for glory, splendour, wealth, or power,
View this inactive state with feverish eyes,
And pleasure they can never taste, despise;
Let them still court that goddess' falser joys,
Who, while she grants their pray'r, their peace destroys.
I envy not the foremost of the great,
Not Walpole's self, directing Europe's fate;
Still let him load ambition's thorny shrine,
Fame be his portion, and contentment mine.
But if the Gods sinister still deny
To live in Ickworth, let me there but die;
Thy hands to close my eyes in Death's long night,
Thy image to attract their latest sight.
Then to the grave attend thy Poet's hearse,
And love his memory as you lov'd his verse.

CONTINUATION,

BY LADY M. W. MONTAGU.

SO sung the poet in a humble strain,
With empty pockets, and a head in pain;
Where the soft clime inclin'd the soul to rest,
And past'ral images inspired the breast.
Apollo listen'd from his heavenly bower,
And, in his health restored, express'd his power.
Pygmalion thus before the Paphian shrine,
With trembling vows address'd the power divine;
Durst hardly make his hopeless wishes known,
And scarce a greater miracle was shewn—
Returning vigour glow'd in ev'ry vein,
And gay ideas flutter in the brain;
Back he returns to breathe his native air,
And all his firm resolves are melted there!

AN EPISTLE

TO THE EARL OF BURLINGTON.

HOW happy you! who varied joys pursue;
And every hour presents you something new!
Plans, schemes, and models, all Palladio's art,
For six long months have gain'd upon your heart;
Of colonnades, of corridores you talk,
The winding stair-case and the cover'd walk;
You blend the orders with Vitruvian toil,
And raise with wond'rous joy the fancy'd pile:
But the dull workman's slow performing hand
But coldly executes his lord's command.
With dirt and mortar soon you grow displeas'd,
Planting succeeds, and avenues are rais'd,
Canals are cut, and mountains level made;
Bowers of retreat, and galleries of shade;
The shaven turf presents a lively green;
The bordering flowers in mystic knots are seen:
With studied art on nature you refine——
The spring beheld you warm in this design,

But scarce the cold attacks your fav'rite trees,
Your inclination fails, and wishes freeze:
You quit the grove so lately you admir'd;
With other views your eager hopes are fir'd,
Post to the city you direct your way;
Not blooming paradise could bribe your stay:
Ambition shews you power's brightest side,
'Tis meanly poor in solitude to hide:
Though certain pains attend the cares of state,
A good man owes his country to be great;
Should act abroad the high-distinguish'd part,
Or shew at least the purpose of his heart.
With thoughts like these the shining courts you seek:
Full of new projects for almost a week;
You then despise the tinsel glittering snare;
Think vile mankind below a serious care.
Life is too short for any distant aim;
And cold the dull reward of future fame:
Be happy then, while yet you have to live;
And love is all the blessing Heav'n can give.
Fir'd by new passion you address the fair;
Survey the opera as a gay parterre:

Young Cloe's bloom had made you certain prize,
But for a side-long glance from Celia's eyes:
Your beating heart acknowledges her power;
Your eager eyes her lovely form devour;
You feel the poison swelling in your breast,
And all your soul by fond desire possess'd.
In dying sighs a long three hours are past;
To some assembly with impatient haste,
With trembling hope, and doubtful fear you move,
Resolv'd to tempt your fate, and own your love:
But there Belinda meets you on the stairs,
Easy her shape, attracting all her airs;
A smile she gives, and with a smile can wound;
Her melting voice has music in the sound;
Her every motion wears resistless grace;
Wit in her mien, and pleasure in her face:
Here while you vow eternity of love,
Cloe and Celia unregarded move.
Thus on the sands of Afric's burning plains,
However deeply made, no long impress remains;
The slightest leaf can leave its figure there;
The strongest form is scatter'd by the air.

So yielding the warm temper of your mind,
So touch'd by every eye, so toss'd by wind;
Oh! how unlike the Heav'n my soul design'd!
Unseen, unheard, the throng around me move;
Not wishing praise, insensible of love:
No whispers soften, nor no beauties fire;
Careless I see the dance, and coldly hear the lyre.

So num'rous herds are driv'n o'er the rock;
No print is left of all the passing flock:
So sings the wind around the solid stone:
So vainly beat the waves with fruitless moan.
Tedious the toil, and great the workman's care,
Who dares attempt to fix impressions there:
But should some swain more skilful than the rest,
Engrave his name upon this marble breast,
Not rolling ages could deface that name;
Thro' all the storms of life 'tis still the same:
Tho' length of years with moss may shade the ground,
Deep, though unseen, remains the secret wound.

VERSES*

ADDRESSED TO THE IMITATOR OF THE FIRST SATIRE OF THE SECOND BOOK OF HORACE.

IN two large columns on thy motly page,
Where Roman wit is strip'd with English rage;
Where ribaldry to satire makes pretence,
And modern scandal rolls with ancient sense:
Whilst on one side we see how Horace thought;
And on the other how he never wrote:
Who can believe, who view the bad, the good,
That the dull copyist better understood
That spirit, he pretends to imitate,
Than heretofore that Greek he did translate?

Thine is just such an image of *his* pen,
As thou thyself art of the sons of men:
Where our own species in burlesque we trace,
A sign-post likeness of the human race;
That is at once resemblance and disgrace.

* These verses are said to have been the joint performance of Lady M. W. Montagu and Lord Hervey, who considered themselves as called upon to reply to Pope's covert Satire.

Horace can laugh, is delicate, is clear;
You only coarsely rail, or darkly sneer:
His style is elegant, his diction pure,
Whilst none thy crabbed numbers can endure;
Hard as thy heart, and as thy birth obscure.*

If *he* has thorns, they all on roses grow;
Thine like rude thistles, and mean brambles show;
With this exception, that tho' rank the soil,
Weeds as they are, they seem produc'd by toil.
Satire should, like a polish'd razor keen,
Wound with a touch, that's scarcely felt or seen.
Thine is an oyster-knife, that hacks and hews;
The rage, but not the talent to abuse:
And is in *hate*, what *love* is in the stews.
'Tis the gross *lust* of hate, that still annoys,
Without distinction, as gross love enjoys:
Neither to folly, nor to vice confin'd;
The object of thy spleen is human-kind:

* This reflection was just. Pope, with all his pretensions to "gentle birth," could not prove the most distant connection with the family of Pope, Earls of Downe, of which he boasted.

It preys on all who yield, or who resist;
To thee 'tis provocation to exist.

But if thou seest * a great and generous heart,
Thy bow is doubly bent to force a dart.
Nor dignity nor innocence is spar'd,
Nor age, nor sex, nor thrones, nor graves, rever'd.
Nor only justice vainly we demand,
But even benefits can't rein thy hand;
To this or that alike in vain we trust,
Nor find thee less ungrateful than unjust.

Not even youth and beauty can controul
The universal rancour of thy soul;
Charms that might soften superstition's rage,
Might humble pride, or thaw the ice of age.
But how should'st thou by beauty's force be mov'd,
No more for loving made than to be lov'd?
It was the equity of righteous Heav'n,
That such a soul to such a form was giv'n;

* TASTE, an Epistle, in which are the reflections upon the Duke of Chandos.

And shews the uniformity of fate,
That one so odious should be born to hate.

When God created thee, one would believe,
He said the same as to the snake of Eve;
To human race antipathy declare,
'Twixt them and thee be everlasting war.
But oh! the sequel of the sentence dread,
And whilst you *bruise their heel*, beware your head.
Nor think thy weakness shall be thy defence,
The female scold's protection in offence.
Sure 'tis as fair to beat who cannot fight,
As 'tis to libel those who cannot write.
And if thou draw'st thy pen to aid the law,
Others a cudgel, or a rod, may draw.
If none with vengeance yet thy crimes pursue,
Or give thy manifold affronts their due;
If limbs unbroken, skin without a stain,
Unwhipt, unblanketed, unkick'd, unslain;
That wretched little carcase you retain,
The reason is, not that the world wants eyes;
But thou'rt so mean, they see, and they despise:

When fretful *porcupine*, with rancorous will,
From mounted back shoots forth a harmless quill,
Cool the spectators stand; and all the while,
Upon the angry little monster smile.
Thus 'tis with thee:—while impotently safe,
You strike unwounding, we unhurt can laugh.
Who but must laugh, this bully when he sees,
A puny insect shiv'ring at a breeze?
One over-match'd by ev'ry blast of wind,
Insulting and provoking all mankind.

Is this the *thing* to keep mankind in awe,
To make those tremble who escape the law?
Is this *the ridicule* to live so long,
The deathless satire, and *immortal song?*
No: like the self-blown praise, thy scandal flies;
And, as we're told of wasps, it stings and dies.

If none do yet return th' intended blow,
You all your safety to your dullness owe:
But whilst that armour thy poor corpse defends,
'Twill make thy readers few, as are thy friends;

Those, who thy nature loath'd, yet lov'd thy art,
Who lik'd thy head, and yet abhor'd thy heart;
Chose thee to read, but never to converse,
And scorn'd in prose, him whom they priz'd in verse;
Even they shall now their partial error see,
Shall shun thy writings like thy company;
And to thy books shall ope their eyes no more
Than to thy person they wou'd do their door.

Nor thou the justice of the world disown,
That leaves thee thus an out-cast, and alone;
For tho' in law, to murder be to kill,
In equity the murder's in the will:
Then whilst with coward hand you stab a name,
And try at least t' assassinate our fame,
Like the first bold assassins be thy lot,
Ne'er be thy guilt forgiven, or forgo;
But as thou hat'st, be hated by mankind,
And with the emblem of thy crooked mind,
Mark'd on thy back, like Cain, by God's own hand,
Wander, like him, accursed through the land.

UNFINISHED SKETCHES OF A LARGER POEM.

NOW, with fresh vigour, morn her light displays,
And the glad birds salute her kindling rays;
The opening buds confess the sun's return,
And rous'd from night all nature seems new-born.
When ponderous dullness slowly wing'd her way,
And with thick fogs oppos'd the rising day.
Phœbus retired as from Thyestes' feast,
Droop'd all the flowers, the aërial musick ceas'd.
Pleas'd with her influence she exults with pride;
"Shall mortals then escape my power? she cried,
Nay in this town where smoke and mists conspire
To cloud the head, and damp the poet's fire,
Shall Addison my empire here dispute,
So justly founded, lov'd, and absolute?
Explode my children, ribaldry and rhyme,
Rever'd from Chaucer's down to Dryden's time?
Distinguish 'twixt false humour and the true,
And wit make lovely to the vulgar view?
No—better things my destiny ordains,
For Oxford has the wand, and Anna reigns."

She ended, and assumed Duke Disney's grin,
With broad plump face, pert eyes, and ruddy skin,
Which shewed the stupid joke which lurk'd
within.

In this lov'd form she knock'd at St. John's*
gate,
Where crowds already for his levee wait;
And wait they may, those wretches that appear
To talk of service past and long arrear:
But the proud partner of his pleasure goes
Thro' crowds of envious eyes and servile bows.
And now approaching where the statesman lay,
To his unwilling eyes revealed the day.
Starting, he wak'd, and waking, swore by God,
This early visit friend is wond'rous odd!
Scarce have I rested full two hours in bed,
And fumes of wine oppress my aching head,
By thee I'm sure my soul is understood,
Too well to plague me for the public good.

* Lord Bolingbroke.

Let stupid patriots toil to serve the brutes,
And waste the fleeting hours in vain disputes.
The use of power supreme I better know,
Nor will I lose the joys the gods bestow;
The sparkling glass, soft flute, and willing fair,
Alternate guard me from the shocks of care.
'Tis the prerogative of wit like mine,
To emulate in ease the pow'rs divine;
And while I revel, leave the busy fools
To plot like chemists, or to drudge like tools.

"Believe me lord! (replies his seeming friend)
Some difficulties every state attend.
Cares must surround the men that wealth possess,
And sorrow mingles ev'n with love's success.
Great as you are no greatness long is sure,
Advancement is but pain if not secure.
All your long schemes may vanish in an hour,
Oh tremble at the sad reverse of pow'r!
How will these slaves that waiting watch your eye
Insulting smile or pass regardless by;

Nor is thought the creature of my fears,
Approaching ruin now most strong appears.
Men must be dull who passively obey,
And ignorance fixes arbitrary sway;
Think of this maxim, and no more permit,
A dangerous* writer to retail his wit.
The consequence of sense is liberty,
And if men think aright they will be free;
Encourage you the poet† I shall bring
Your Granville he already tries to sing;
Nor think, my Lord, I only recommend
An able author, but an useful friend;
In verse his phlegm, in puns he shews his fire,
And skill'd in pimping to your heart's desire."

"I thank thee Duke (replies the drowsy peer)
But cannot listen to thy childish fear.
This Addison, 'tis true, debauch'd in schools,
Will sometimes oddly talk of musty rules.

* Alluding to the Spectator, at that time publishing.

† Pope.

Yet here and there I see a master line,
I feel and I confess the power divine.
In spite of interest charm'd into applause,
I wish for such a champion in our cause:
Nor shall your reasons force me to submit
To patronise a bard of meaner wit;
Men can but say wit did my judgment blind,
And wit's the noblest frailty of the mind."

The disappointed goddess swell'd with spite,
Dropping her borrow'd form, appears in open light.
So the sly nymph in masquerade disguise,
The faith of her suspected lover tries;
But when the perjury too plain appears,
Her eyes are fill'd with mingled rage and tears:
No more remembers the affected tone,
Sinks the feign'd voice, and thunders in her own.

"How hast thou dared my party then to quit,
Or dost thou, wretch, presume thou art a wit?
Read thy own works, consider well each line,
In each dull page, how palpably I shine!

'Tis me that to thy eloquence affords,
Such empty thoughts wrapt in superfluous words;
To me alone your pamphlet-praise you owe,
'Tis I your tropes and florid sense bestow;
After such wreaths bestow'd, such service done,
Dare you refuse protection to my son?
The time shall come, tho' now at court ador'd,
When still a writer, tho' no more a lord.
On common stalls thy darling works be spread,
And thou shalt answer them to make them read."

She said, and turning showed her wrinkled neck,
In scales and colour like a roach's back.

THE COURT OF DULLNESS,

A FRAGMENT.

* * * * * * * *

* * * * * * * *

HER palace plac'd beneath a muddy road,
And such the influence of the dull abode,
The carrier's horse above can scarcely drag his load.
Here chose the goddess her belov'd retreat,*
Which Phœbus tries in vain to penetrate,
Adorn'd within with shells of small expence,
(Emblems of tinsel rhyme and trifling sense)
Perpetual fogs enclose the sacred cave,
The neighbouring sinks their fragrant odours gave,
In contemplation here she passed her hours,
Closely attended by subservient powers:
Bold prophanation with a brazen brow,
Much to this great ally does dullness owe:
But still more near the goddess you attend
Naked obscenity! her darling friend.

* Alluding to Pope's grotto at Twickenham.

To thee for shelter all the dull still fly,
Pert double meanings e'en at school we try,
What numerous writers owe their praise to thee,
No sex—no age—is from thy influence free ;
By thee how bright appears the senseless song,
By thee the book is sold, the lines are strong,
The heaviest poet, by thy powerful aid,
Warms the brisk youth and charms the sprightly maid ;
Where breathes the mortal who's not prov'd thy force
In well bred pun or waiting-room discourse ?

Such were the chiefs who form'd her gloomy court,
Her pride, her ornament and her support,
Behind attended such a numerous crowd
Of quibbles strain'd, old rhymes and laughter loud,
Throngs that might even make a goddess proud.
Yet pensive thoughts lay brooding in her breast,
And fear, the mate of power, her mind oppress'd,

Oft she revolv'd—for oh too well she knew,
What Merlin sung and part long since prov'd true,
" When Harry's brows the diadem adorn,
From reformation learning shall be born?
Slowly in strength the infant shall improve
The parent's glory and its country's love:
Free from the thraldom of monastic rhymes,
In bright progression bless succeeding times;
Milton free po'sy from the monkish chain,
And Addison that Milton shall explain;
Point out the beauties of each living page;
Reform the taste of a degen'rate age;
Shew that true wit disdains all little art,
And can at once engage and mend the heart;
Knows even popular applause to gain,
Yet not malicious, wanton, or prophane."

This prophecy perplex'd her anx'ous head;
And, yawning thrice, thus to her sons she said:
When such an author honored shall appear
'Tis plain, the hour of our destruction's near;

And public rumour now aloud proclaims
At universal monarchy he aims.
What to this hero, whom shall we oppose,
A strong confederacy of stupid foes—
Such brave allies as are by nature fit
To check the progress of o'erflowing wit.
Where envy and where impudence are join'd
To contradict the voice of humankind.
At Dacier's ignorance shall gravely smile,
And blame the coarseness of Spectator's style;
Shall swear that Tickell understands not Greek,
That Addison can't write, nor Walpole speak.

Fir'd by this project Prophanation rose—
"One Leader, Goddess, let me here propose;
In a near realm, which owns thy gentle sway,
My darling son now chaunts his pleasing lay,
Trampling on order, decency, and laws,
And vaunts himself the champion of my cause.
Him will I bring to teach the callow youth
To scorn dry morals—laugh at sacred truth,

All fears of future reckonings he shall quench,
And bid them bravely drink and freely wench.
By his example much, by precept more,
They learn 'tis wit to swear, and safe to wh—re.

* * * * * * * * * * *

Mocks Newton's schemes, and Tillotson's dis-
course,
And imitates the virtues of a horse.
With this design to add to his renown,
He wears the rev'rend dress of band and gown.*
The Goddess, pleas'd, bestow'd a gracious grin,
When thus does fair Obscenity begin:
"My humbler subjects are not plac'd so high,
They joke in kitchens, and in cellars ply;
Yet one I have, bred in those worthy schools,
Admir'd by shoals of male and female fools;
In ballads what I dictate, he shall sing,
And troops of converts to my banners bring.
Bold in my cause, and most prophanely dull,
With smooth unmeaning rhimes the towns shall
lull;

* This Character is drawn for Dr. Swift.

Shall sing of worms in great Arbuthnot's strain,
In lewd burlesque the sacred Psalms prophane;
To Maids of Honour songs obscene address,
Nor need we doubt his wonderful success.
Long have I watch'd this genius yet unknown,
Inspir'd his rhyme, and mark'd him for my own;
His early youth in superstition bred,
And monkish legends all the books he read.
Tinctur'd by these, proceeds his love of rhyme,
Milton he scorns, but crambo thinks divine.
And oh! 'tis sure (our foes confess this truth)
The old Crambonians yield to this stupendous youth.
But present want obscures the poet's name,
Be it my charge to talk him into fame.
My Lansdowne, (whose love songs so smoothly run;
My darling author, and my fav'rite son)
He shall protect the man* whom I inspire,
And Windsor-forest openly admire;

* Mr. Pope.

And Bolingbroke, with flatt'ry shall bribe,
'Till the charm'd lord most nobly shall subscribe;
And hostile Addison too late shall find,
'Tis easier to corrupt than mend mankind.
The town, which now revolts, once more obey,
And the whole island own my pristine sway;"
She said, and slowly leaves the realms of night,
While the curs'd phantoms praise her droning
flight.

AN EPISTLE

FROM POPE TO LORD BOLINGBROKE.

CONFESS, dear Lælius! * pious, just, and wise,
Some self-content does in that bosom rise,
When you reflect, as sure you sometimes must,
What talents Heaven does to thy virtue trust,
While with contempt you view poor human-kind,
Weak, wilful, sensual, passionate, and blind.
Amid these errors thou art faultless found,
(The moon takes lustre from the darkness round)
Permit me too, a small attendant star,
To twinkle, tho' in a more distant sphere;
Small things with great, we Poets oft compare.
With admiration all your steps I view,
And almost envy what I can't pursue.
The world must grant, and ('tis no common fame)
My courage and my probity the same;

* Pope first addressed his Essay on Man to Lord Bolingbroke, as Lælius.

But you, great Lord, to nobler scenes were born;
Your early youth did Anna's court adorn.
Let Oxford own, let Catalonia tell,
What various victims to your wisdom fell;
Let vows or benefits the vulgar bind,
Such ties can never chain th' intrepid mind.
Recorded be that memorable hour,
When, to elude exasperated pow'r,
With blushless front, you durst your friend betray,
Advise the whole confederacy to stay,
While with sly courage you run brisk away.
By a deserted court with joy receiv'd
Your projects all admir'd, your oaths believ'd;
Some trust obtain'd, of which good use you made,
To gain a pardon where you first betray'd.
But what is pardon to th' aspiring breast?
You shou'd have been First Minister at least:
Failing of that, forsaking and depress'd,
Sure any soul but your's had sought for rest;
And mourn'd in shades, far from the public eye,
Successless fraud, and useless infamy.

And here, my Lord! let all mankind admire
The bold efforts of unexhausted fire;
You stand the champion of the people's cause,
And bid the mob reform defective laws.
Oh! was your pow'r, like your intention, good!
Your native land wou'd stream with civic blood.
I own these glorious schemes I view with pain;
My little mischiefs to myself seem mean.
Such ills are humble tho' my heart is great,
All I can do is flatter, lie, and cheat;
Yet I may say 'tis plain that you preside
O'er all my morals, and 'tis much my pride
To tread with steps unequal where you guide.
My first subscribers,* I have first defam'd,
And when detected, never was asham'd;
Rais'd all the storms I could in private life,
Whisper'd the husband to reform the wife;
Outwitted Lintot in his very trade,
And charity with obloquy repaid.
Yet while you preach'd in prose, I scold in rhymes,
Against the injustice of flagitious times.

* To the Translation of Homer.

You, learned Doctor of the public stage,
Give gilded poison to corrupt the age;
Your poor toad-cater I, around me scatter
My scurril jests, and gaping crowds bespatter.
This may seem envy to the formal fools,
Who talk of virtue's bounds and honour's rules;
We, who with piercing eyes look nature through,
We know that all is right, in all we do.

Reason's erroneous—honest instinct right—
Monkeys were made to grin and fleas to bite.
Using the spite by the Creator given,
We only tread the path that's mark'd by Heaven.
And sure with justice 'tis that we exclaim,
Such wrongs must e'en your modesty inflame;
While blockheads, court-rewards and honours share,
You, poet, patriot, and philosopher,
No bills in pocket, nor no garter wear.

When I see smoking on a booby's board,
Fat Ortolans and pye of Perigord,

Myself am mov'd to high poetic rage,
(The Homer and the Horace of the age)
Puppies who have the insolence to dine
With smiling beauties, and with sparkling wine.
While I retire, plagu'd with an empty purse,
Eat broccoli, and kiss my ancient nurse.
But had we flourish'd when stern Harry reign'd,
Our good designs had been but ill explain'd;
The axe had cut your solid reas'nings short,
I, in the porter's lodge, been scourg'd at court.
To better times kind Heav'n reserv'd our birth,
Happy for you such coxcombs are on earth!
Mean spirits seek their villainy to hide;
We show our venom'd souls with nobler pride,
And in bold strokes have all mankind defy'd.
Past o'er the bounds that keep mankind in awe,
And laugh'd at justice, liberty, and law.
While our admirers stare with dumb surprize,
Treason and scandal we monopolize.
Yet this remains our more peculiar boast,
You 'scape the block, and I the whipping-post.

LADY HERTFORD

TO LORD WILLIAM HAMILTON.

DEAR Colin prevent my warm blushes,
Since how can I speak without pain?
My eyes oft' have told you my wishes,
Why don't you their meaning explain?

My passion will lose by expression,
And you may too cruelly blame;
Then do not expect a confession,
Of what is too tender to name.

Since your's is the province of speaking,
How can you then hope it from me?
Our wishes should be in our keeping,
'Till your's tell us what they would be.

Alas! then why don't you discover?
Did your heart feel such torments as mine,
Eyes need not tell over and over,
What I in my breast would confine.

ANSWERED, FOR LORD WILLIAM HAMILTON,

BY LADY M. W. MONTAGU.

GOOD Madam, when ladies are willing,
A man must needs look like a fool;
For me, I would not give a shilling
For one who would love out of rule.

You should leave us to guess by your blushing,
And not speak the matter so plain;
'Tis our's to write and be pushing,
'Tis your's to affect a disdain.

That you are in a terrible taking,
By all these sweet oglings I see;
But the fruit that can fall without shaking,
Indeed is too mellow for me.

EPISTLE

FROM ARTHUR GREY, THE FOOTMAN,*

TO Mrs. MAHONEY,

AFTER HIS CONDEMNATION FOR ATTEMPTING TO COMMIT VIOLENCE.

READ, lovely nymph, and tremble not to read,
I have no more to wish, nor you to dread;
I ask not life, for life to me were vain,
And death a refuge from severer pain.
My only hope in these last lines I try;
I would be pitied, and I then would die.

Long had I liv'd as sordid as my fate,
Nor curs'd the destiny that made me wait
A servile slave: content with homely food,
The gross instinct of happiness pursu'd:
Youth gave me sleep at night, and warmth of blood.

* This man was tried for the offence in 1721. As the lady had wrested the pistol from his hand, and alarmed the family, he was convicted only of burglary, and transported.

Ambition yet had never touch'd my breast;
My lordly master knew no sounder rest;
With labour healthy, in obedience blest.
But when I saw——oh! had I never seen
That wounding softness, that engaging mien!
The mist of wretched education flies,
Shame, fear, desire, despair, and love, arise,
The new creation of those beauteous eyes.
But yet that love pursu'd no guilty aim,
Deep in my heart I hid the secret flame.
I never hop'd my fond desire to tell,
And all my wishes were to serve you well.
Heav'ns! how I flew, when wing'd by your command,
And kiss'd the letters giv'n me by your hand.
How pleas'd, how proud, how fond was I to wait,
Present the sparkling wine, or change the plate!
How when you sung my soul devour'd the sound,
And ev'ry sense was in the rapture drown'd!
Tho' bid to go, I quite forgot to move;
——You knew not that stupidity was love!

But oh! the torment not to be express'd,
The grief, the rage, the hell, that fir'd this breast,
When my great rivals, in embroid'ry gay,
Sate by your side, or led you from the play!
I still contriv'd near as I could to stand,
(The flambeau trembling in my shaking hand)
I saw, or thought I saw, those fingers press'd,
For thus their passion by my own I guess'd,
And jealous fury all my soul possess'd.
Like torrents, love and indignation meet,
And madness would have thrown me at your feet.
Turn, lovely nymph (for so I would have said)
Turn from those triflers who make love a trade;
This is true passion in my eyes you see;
They cannot—no, they cannot—love like me.
Frequent debauch has pall'd their sickly taste,
Faint their desire, and in a moment past:
They sigh not from the heart, but from the brain;
Vapours of vanity and strong Champagne.
Too dull to feel what forms, like your's, inspire,
After long talking of their painted fire,
To some lewd brothel they at night retire;

There pleas'd with fancy'd quality and charms,
Enjoy your beauties in a strumpet's arms.
Such are the joys those toasters have in view,
And such the wit and pleasure they pursue:
——And is this love that ought to merit you?
Each opera-night a new address begun,
They swear to thousands what they swear to one.
Not thus I sigh—but all my sighs are vain—
Die, wretched Arthur, and conceal thy pain:
'Tis impudence to wish, and madness to complain.

Fix'd on this view, my only hope of ease,
I waited not the aid of slow disease;
The keenest instruments of death I sought,
And death alone employ'd my lab'ring thought.
This all the night—when I remember well,
The charming tinkle of your morning bell!
Fir'd by the sound, I hasten'd with your tea,
With one last look to smooth the darksome way.—
But oh! how dear that fatal look has cost!
In that fond moment my resolves were lost.

Hence all my guilt, and all your sorrows rise—
I saw the languid softness of your eyes;
I saw the dear disorder of your bed;
Your cheeks all glowing with a tempting red;
Your night-cloaths tumbled with resistless grace,
Your flowing hair play'd careless down your face,
Your night-gown fasten'd with a single pin;
—Fancy improv'd the wond'rous charms within!
I fix'd my eyes upon that heaving breast,
And hardly, hardly, I forbore the rest;
Eager to gaze, unsatisfied with sight,
My head grew giddy with the near delight!
—Too well you know the fatal following night!
Th' extremest proof of my desire I give,
And since you will not love, I will not live.
Condemn'd by you, I wait the righteous doom,
Careless and fearless of the woes to come.
But when you see me waver in the wind,
My guilty flame extinct, my soul resign'd,
Sure you may pity what you can't approve,
The cruel consequence of furious love.

Think the bold wretch, that could so greatly dare,
Was tender, faithful, ardent, and sincere:
Think when I held the pistol to your breast,
Had I been of the world's large rule possess'd,
That world had then been your's, and I been blest;
Think that my life was quite below my care,
Nor fear'd I any hell beyond despair.——

If these reflections, though they seize you late,
Give some compassion for your Arthur's fate:
Enough you give, nor ought I to complain;
You pay my pangs, nor have I dy'd in vain.

THE FOURTH ODE

OF THE FIRST BOOK OF HORACE, IMITATED.

"Solvitur acris hyems grata vice veris," &c.

SHARP winter now dissolved, the linnets sing,
The grateful breath of pleasing Zephyrs bring
The welcome joys of long desired spring,

The gallies now for open sea prepare,
The herds forsake their stalls for balmy air,
The fields adorn'd with green th' approaching sun
declare

In shining nights the charming Venus leads
Her troop of Graces, and her lovely maids
Who gaily trip the ground in myrtle shades,

The blazing forge her husband Vulcan heats,
And thunderlike the labouring hammer beats,
While toiling Cyclops every stroke repeats.

Of myrtle new the chearful wreath compose,
Or various flowers which opening spring bestows,
Till coming June presents the blushing rose.

Pay your vow'd offering to God Faunus' bower!
Then, happy Sestius, seize the present hour,
'Tis all that nature leaves to mortal power.

The equal hand of strong impartial fate,
Levels the peasant and th' imperious great,
Nor will that doom on human projects wait.

To the dark mansions of the senseless dead,
With daily steps our destined path we tread,
Realms still unknown, of which so much is said.

Ended your schemes of pleasure and of pride,
In joyous feasts no one will there preside,
Torn from your Lycida's beloved side.

Whose tender youth does now our eyes engage,
And soon will give in his maturer age,
Sighs to our virgins—to our matron's rage.

THE FIFTH ODE

OF THE FIRST BOOK OF HORACE, IMITATED.

"Quis multâ gracilis te puer in rosa."

FOR whom are now your airs put on,
And what new beauty's doom'd to be undone?
  That careless elegance of dress,
This essence that perfumes the wind,
  Your very motion does confess
Some secret conquest is design'd.

Alas! the poor unhappy maid,
To what a train of ills betray'd!
  What fears, what pangs, shall rend her breast,
How will her eyes dissolve in tears!
  That now with glowing joy is bless'd,
Charm'd with the faithless vows she hears.

So the young sailor on the summer sea,
Gaily pursues his destin'd way:

Fearless and careless on the deck he stands,
Till sudden storms arise and thunders roll;
In vain he cast his eyes to distant lands,
Distracting terror tears his timorous soul.

For me, secure I view the raging main,
Past are my dangers, and forgot my pain:
My votive tablet in the temple shews
The monument of folly past;
I paid the bounteous god my grateful vows,
Who snatch'd from ruin, sav'd me at the last.

THE LOVER:

A BALLAD.

TO MR. CONGREVE.

I.

At length, by so much importunity press'd,
Take, Congreve, at once the inside of my breast.
This stupid indiff'rence so often you blame,
Is not owing to nature, to fear, or to shame:
I am not as cold as a virgin in lead,
Nor is Sunday's sermon so strong in my head:
I know but too well how time flies along,
That we live but few years, and yet fewer are
young.

II.

But I hate to be cheated, and never will buy
Long years of repentance for moments of joy.
Oh! was there a man (but where shall I find
Good sense and good-nature so equally join'd?)

Would value his pleasure, contribute to mine;
Not meanly would boast, nor lewdly design;
Not over severe, yet not stupidly vain,
For I would have the power, tho' not give the pain.

III.

No pedant, yet learned; no rake-helly gay,
Or laughing, because he has nothing to say;
To all my whole sex obliging and free,
Yet never be fond of any but me;
In public preserve the decorum that's just,
And shew in his eyes he is true to his trust;
Then rarely approach, and respectfully bow,
But not fulsomely pert, nor foppishly low.

IV.

But when the long hours of public are past,
And we meet with Champagne and a chicken at last,
May every fond pleasure that moment endear;
Be banish'd afar both discretion and fear!

Forgetting or scorning the airs of the crowd,
He may cease to be formal, and I to be proud,
'Till lost in the joy, we confess that we live,
And he may be rude, and yet I may forgive.

V.

And that my delight may be solidly fix'd,
Let the friend and the lover be handsomely mix'd,
In whose tender bosom my soul may confide,
Whose kindness can sooth me, whose counsel can
guide.
From such a dear lover as here I describe,
No danger should fright me, no millions should
bribe;
But till this astonishing creature I know,
As I long have liv'd chaste, I will keep myself so.

VI.

I never will share with the wanton coquet,
Or be caught by a vain affectation of wit.
The toasters and songsters may try all their art,
But never shall enter the pass of my heart.

I loath the lewd rake, the dress'd fopling despise:
Before such pursuers the nice virgin flies:
And as Ovid has sweetly in parable told,
We harden like trees, and like rivers grow cold.

ON SEEING

A PORTRAIT OF SIR ROBERT WALPOLE

SUCH were the lively eyes and rosy hue
Of Robin's face, when Robin first I knew;
The gay companion and the favourite guest;
Lov'd without awe, and without views caress'd;
His cheerful smile, and open honest look,
Added new graces to the truth he spoke.
Then, every man found something to commend,
The pleasant neighbour, and the worthy friend.
The generous master of a private house,
The tender father and indulgent spouse.

The hardest censors at the worst believ'd,
His temper was too easily deceiv'd;
(A consequential ill good-nature draws,
A bad effect, but from a noble cause)
Whence then these clamours of a judging crowd?
Suspicious, griping, insolent and proud—
Rapacious, cruel, violent, unjust;
False to his friend, and traitor to his trust!

AN ELEGY

ON MRS. THOMPSON.*

UNHAPPY fair! by fatal love betray'd!
Must then thy beauties thus untimely fade?
And all thy blooming, soft, inspiring charms,
Become a prey to death's destructive arms?
Tho' short thy day, and transient like the wind,
How far more blest than those yet left behind!
Safe in the grave, thy griefs with thee remain;
And life's tempestuous billows break in vain.
Ye tender nymphs in lawless pastimes gay,
Who heedless down the paths of pleasure stray;
Tho' long secure, with blissful joy elate,
Yet pause, and think of Arabella's fate:
For such may be your unexpected doom,
And your next pleasures lull you in the tomb.
But let it be the Muse's gentle care
To shield from envy's rage the mould'ring fair:

* Arabella, the wife of Edward Thompson, Esq. one of the daughters and co-heirs of Edmund Dunch, Esq. The others were the Duchess of Manchester and Lady Oxenden.

To draw a veil o'er faults she can't defend;
And what prudes have devour'd, leave time to end:
Be it her part to drop a pitying tear,
And mourning sigh around thy sable bier.
Nor shall thy woes long glad th' ill-natured croud,
Silent to praise, and in detraction loud:
When scandal, that thro' life each worth destroys,
And malice that imbitters all our joys,
Shall in some ill-starr'd wretch find later stains;
And let thine rest, forgot as thy remains.

ON THE DEATH OF MRS. BOWES.

WRITTEN EXTEMPORE ON A CARD, IN A LARGE COMPANY, DECEMBER 14, 1724.

HAIL happy bride, for thou art truly blest!
Three months of rapture, crown'd with endless rest.
Merit, like your's, was Heav'ns peculiar care,
You lov'd—yet tasted happiness sincere.
To you the sweets of love were only shewn,
The sure succeeding bitter dregs unknown;
You had not yet the fatal change deplor'd,
The tender lover, for the imperious lord:
Nor felt the pain that jealous fondness brings;
Nor felt the coldness, from possession springs,
Above your sex, distinguish'd in your fate,
You trusted—yet experienc'd no deceit;
Soft were your hours, and wing'd with pleasure flew;
No vain repentance gave a sigh to you:
And if superior bliss Heaven can bestow,
With fellow-angels you enjoy it now.

A MAN IN LOVE.

"L'Homme qui ne se trouve point & ne se trouvera jamais."

THE man who feels the dear disease,
Forgets himself, neglects to please:
The crowd avoids and seeks the groves,
And much he thinks when much he loves;
Press'd with alternate hope and fear,
Sighs in her absence, sighs when she is near.
The gay, the fond, the fair, the young,
Those trifles pass unseen along;
To him a pert, insipid throng.
But most he shuns the vain coquet;
Contemns her false affected wit:
The minstrels sound, the flowing bowl,
Oppress and hurt the amorous soul.
'Tis solitude alone can please,
And give some intervals of ease.
He feeds the soft distemper there,
And fondly courts the distant fair;

To balls, the silent shade prefers,
And hates all other charms but her's.
When thus your absent swain can do,
Molly, you may believe him true.

A BALLAD.

TO THE TUNE OF "THE IRISH HOWL."

I.

TO that dear nymph, whose pow'rful name
Does every throbbing nerve inflame,
(As the soft sound I low repeat
My pulse unequal measures beat)
Whose eyes I never more shall see,
That once so sweetly shin'd on thee;
Go, gentle wind! and kindly bear
My tender wishes to the fair.

Hoh, ho, ho, &c.

II.

Amidst her pleasures let her know
The secret anguish of my woe,
The midnight pang, the zealous hell,
Does in this tortured bosom dwell:
While laughing she, and full of play,
Is with her young companions gay;
Or hearing in some fragrant bower
Her lover's sigh, and beauty's power.

Hoh, ho, ho, &c.

III.

Lost and forgotten may I be!
Oh may no pitying thought of me
Disturb the joy that she may find,
When love is crown'd, and fortune kind:
May that bless'd swain (whom yet I hate)
Be proud of his distinguish'd fate:
Each happy night be like the first;
And he be bless'd as I am curs'd.
Hoh, ho, ho, &c.

IV.

While in these pathless woods I stray,
And lose my solitary way;
Talk to the stars, to trees complain,
And tell the senseless woods my pain:
But madness spares the sacred name,
Nor dares the hidden wound proclaim;
Which secret rankling, sure and slow,
Shall close in endless peace my woe.
Hoh, ho, ho, &c.

V.

When this fond heart shall ake no more,
And all the ills of life are o'er;
(If gods by lovers prayers are mov'd,
As ev'ry god in heaven has lov'd)
Instead of bright Elysian joys,
That unknown something in the skies,
In recompence of all my pain,
The only heaven I'd obtain,
May I, the guardian of her charms,
Preserve that paradise from harms.

Hoh, ho, ho, &c.

A HYMN TO THE MOON.

WRITTEN IN JULY, IN AN ARBOR.

THOU silver Deity of secret night,
  Direct my footsteps thro' the woodland shade;
Thou conscious witness of unknown delight,
  The Lover's guardian, and the Muse's aid!
By thy pale beams I solitary rove,
  To thee my tender grief confide;
Serenely sweet you gild the silent grove,
  My friend, my goddess, and my guide.
E'en thee, fair queen, from thy amazing height,
  The charms of young Endymion drew;
Veil'd with the mantle of concealing night;
  With all thy greatness, and thy coldness too*.

* This sonnet is preserved by Count Algarotti in the seventh Volume of his works, and mentioned with great commendation.

TRANSLATED BY HERSELF.

DELLA notte serena argentea Diva,
Testimon fido d' piaceri ignoti ;
Custode degli amanti e delle Muse
Fautrice, reggi me ne' boschi oscuri,
Da' suoi pallidi rai scorto io camino,
Su la verra ed a ve svelo i piu cupi,
Pensieri. Ah indora il tacitorno bosco ;
Dolcemente serena amica mia
E mia guida, e mia Dea. Bella reina
Tu della sua prodigiosa altezza
Il lusinghiero Endimione attrae,
Del velo ingombra della notre oscura,
Della tua ampiezza in onta e del tuo gelo,

THE BRIDE IN THE COUNTRY;

A PARODY ON ROWE'S BALLAD,

"DESPAIRING BESIDE A CLEAR STREAM," &c.

BY the side of a half-rotten wood
Melantha sate silently down,
Convinc'd that her scheme was not good,
And vex'd to be absent from town.
Whilst pit'ed by no living soul,
To herself she was forc'd to reply,
And the sparrow, as grave as an owl,
Sate list'ning and pecking hard by.

II.

"Alas! silly maid that I was;"
Thus sadly complaining, she cry'd;
"When first I forsook that dear place,
'T had been better by far I had died!
How gayly I pass'd the long days,
In a round of continu'd delights!
Park, visits, assemblies, and plays,
And a dance to enliven the nights.

III.

" How simple was I to believe
Delusive poetical dreams!
Or the flattering landscapes they give,
Of meadows and murmuring streams.
Bleak mountains, and cold starving rocks,
Are the wretched result of my pains;
The swains greater brutes than their flocks,
And the nymphs as polite as the swains.

IV.

" What tho' I have got my dear Phil;
I see him all night and all day;
I find I must not have my will,
And I've cursedly sworn to obey!
Fond damsel thy pow'r is lost,
As now I experience too late;
Whatever a lover may boast,
A husband is what one may hate!

V.

" And thou, my old woman, so dear,
My all that is left of relief,
Whatever I suffer, forbear—
Forbear to dissuade me from grief;
'Tis in vain, as you say, to repine
At ills which cannot be redress'd;
But, in sorrows so poignant as mine,
To be patient, alas! is a jest.

VI.

" If, farther to soothe my distress,
Your tender compassion is led,
Come hither and help to undress,
And decently put me to bed.
The last humble solace I wait,
Wou'd Heav'n but indulge me the boon,
May some dream, less unkind than my fate,
In a vision, transport me to town.

VII.

" Clarissa, meantime, weds a beau,
Who decks her in golden array ;
She's the finest at ev'ry fine shew,
And flaunts it at Park and at Play :
Whilst I am here left in the lurch,
Forgot, and secluded from view ;
Unless when some bumkin at church
Stares wistfully over the pew :

SONG.

WHY should you think I live unpleas'd,
Because I am not pleas'd with you,
My mind is not so far diseas'd,
To yield when powder'd fops pursue.

My vanity can find no charm
In common prostituted vows;
Nor can you raise a wish that's warm
In one that your true value knows.

While cold and careless thus I shun
The buz and flutter that you make,
Perhaps some giddy girl may run
To catch the prize that I forsake.

So brightly shines the glittering glare,
In unexperienc'd children's eyes,
When they with little arts ensnare
The gaudy painted butterflies.

While they with pride the conquest boast,
  And think the chase deserving care,
Those scorn the useless toil they cost
  Who're us'd to more substantial fare.

SONG.—RONDEAU.

FINISH these languors! Oh I'm sick!
Of dying airs I know the trick.
Long since I've learn'd to well explain
The unmeaning cant of fire and pain,
And see thro' all the senseless lies
Of burning darts from killing eyes;
I'm tir'd with this continual rout
Of bowing low, and leading out.
Finish, &c.

Finish this tedious dangling trade,
By which so many fools are made;
For fools they are, whom you can please
By such affected airs as these:
At opera near my box to stand,
And slyly press the given hand,
Thus may you wait whole years in vain;
But sure you would, were you in pain.
Finish, &c.

EPITHALAMIUM.

SINCE you, Mr. H**d, will marry black
Kate,
Accept of good wishes for that blessed state:
May you fight all the day like a dog and a cat,
And yet ev'ry year produce a new brat.
Fal la!

May she never be honest—you never be sound;
May her tongue like a clapper be heard a mile
round;
Till abandon'd by joy, and deserted by grace,
You hang yourselves both in the very same place.
Fal la!

THE NINTH ODE

OF THE THIRD BOOK OF HORACE, IMITATED, 1736.

"Donec gratus eram tibi."

SIR ROBERT WALPOLE.

WHILST in each of my schemes you most heartily join'd,
And help'd the worst jobs that I ever design'd,
In pamphlets, in ballads, in senate, at table,
Thy satire was witty, thy counsel was able.

WILLIAM PULTENEY.

Whilst with me you divided both profit and care,
And the plunder and glory did equally share;
Assur'd of his place, if my fat friend should die,
The Prince of Wales was not so happy as I.

SIR ROBERT WALPOLE.

Harry Pelham is now my support and delight,
Whom we bubble all day and we joke on at night;
His head is well furnish'd, his lungs have their merit,
I would venture a rope to advance such a spirit.

WILLIAM PULTENEY.

I too have a Harry more useful than your's,
Writes verses like mad, and will talk you whole
hours;
I would bleed by the hatchet, or swing by the cord,
To see him once more in his robes, like a lord.

SIR ROBERT WALPOLE.

But what if this quarrel was kindly made up,
Would you, my dear Willy accept of a sup?
If the Queen should confess you had long been her
choice,
And you knew it was I who had spoke in her voice?

WILLIAM PULTENEY.

Tho' my Harry's so gay, so polite, and so civil,
You rude as a bear, and more proud than the Devil;
I gladly would drop him, and laugh in your ear
At the fools we have made, for this last dozen year.

A SUMMARY OF

LORD LYTTLETON's

ADVICE TO A LADY.

"The counsels of a friend, Belinda, hear, &c."

Be plain in dress, and sober in your diet,
In short, my deary, kiss me! and be quiet.

SONG.

WHY will Delia thus retire,
And languish life away,
While the sighing crowds admire,
'Tis too soon for hartshorn tea.

All these dismal looks and fretting
Cannot Damon's life restore;
Long ago the worms have eat him,
You can never see him more.

Once again consult your toilet,
In the glass your face review;
So much weeping sure will spoil it,
And no spring your charms renew.

I, like you, was born a woman,
Well I know what vapours mean;
The disease alas is common,
Single we have all the spleen.

All the morals that they teach us
Never cured sorrow yet:
Choose among the pretty fellows,
One of humour, youth, and wit.

Prithee hear him ev'ry morning,
At the least an hour or two;
Once again at night returning,
I believe the dose will do.

THE SAME,

TRANSLATED BY LADY M. W. MONTAGU.

Recipe per l'Excellentissima Signora Chiara Michelli.

Vi consigliate con lo specchio, e il vostro,
Viso mirate—lagrime cotanti
Lo guasteranno, ed i perduti vezzi
Non avranno altra primavera. Io nacqui
Donna qual voi e so qual voi le forza,
Che hanno i vapori e infirmita commune,
Tutte abbiam mal di milza, e non sanaro,
Delle moral le massime piu saggi
Gli minomi neppur de' nostri guai.
Il piu amabile voi tra tanti amanti,
Sceglier vi piaccia, e sopra tutto quello
Chi piu degli altri ha gioventude e spirito,
Jo vi prego d'udirlo un ora al giorno,
Ed un altra la sera, e questa dose
Sia bastante rimedio al vostra male.

THE POLITICIANS.

IN ancient days when ev'ry brute
To human privilege had right;
Could reason, wrangle, or dispute,
As well as scratch, and tear, and bite.

When Phœbus shone his brightest ray,
The rip'ning corn his pow'r confess'd;
His cheering beams made Nature gay,
The eagle in his warmth was blest.

But mal-contents e'en then arose,
The birds who love the dolesome night;
The darkest grove with care they chose,
And there caball'd against the light.

The screech-owl, with ill-boding cry,
Portends strange things, old women say:
Stops ev'ry fool that passes by,
And frights the school-boy from his play.

The raven and the double bat,
With families of owls combine;
In close consult they rail and chat,
And curse aloud the glorious shine.

While the great planet, all serene,
Heedless pursues his destin'd way;
He asks not what these murmurs mean,
But runs his course, and gives us day.

BALLAD, ON A LATE OCCURRENCE.

AMONG LADY M. W. MONTAGU'S MSS.

I.

UNGODLY papers ev'ry week
Poor simple souls persuade,
That courtiers good for nothing are,
Or but for mischief made.

II.

But I, who know their worthy hearts,
Pronounce that we are blind;
Who disappoint their honest schemes,
Who would be just and kind.

III.

For in this vile degen'rate age,
'Tis dang'rous to do good;
Which will, when I have told my tale,
Be better understood.

IV.

A puppy, gamesome, blithe, and young,
Who play'd about the court,
Was destined by unlucky boys,
To be their noon-day's sport.

V.

With flatt'ring words they him entic'd,
(Words such as much prevail)
And then with cruel art they ty'd
A bottle to his tail.

VI.

Lord Hervey at a window stood,
Detesting of the fact;
And cried aloud with all his might,
" I know the bottle's crack'd.

VII.

" Do not to such a dirty hole
Let them your tail apply;
Alas! you cannot know these things
One half so well as I.

VIII.

"Harmless and young, you don't suspect
The venom of this deed;
But I see thro' the whole design,
It is to make you bleed."

IX.

This good advice was cast away;
The puppy saw it shine;
And tamely lick'd their treach'rous hands,
And thought himself grown fine.

X.

But long he had not worn the gem,
But, as Lord Hervey said,
He ran and bled, the more he ran,
Alas! the more he bled.

XI.

Griev'd to the soul, this gallant Lord
Tripp'd hastily down stairs,
With courage and compassion fir'd,
To set him free prepares

XII.

But such was his ingratitude
To this most noble Lord;
He bit his lily hand quite through,
As he untied the cord.

XIII.

Next day, the Maids of Honour came,
As I heard people tell;
They wash'd the wound with brinish tears,
—And yet it is not well.

XIV.

Oh! gen'rous youth, my counsel take,
And warlike acts forbear;
Put on white gloves, and lead folks out,
—For that is your affair.*

XV.

Never attempt to take away
Bottles from others' tails,
For that is what no soul will bear
From Italy to Wales.

* Lord Hervey was at that time Vice Chamberlain.

SONG.

I.

BLAME not that love too cruel fair,
Which your own charms did first create;
Blame not my silence and despair,
Such crimes can ne'er deserve your hate:
Why should your eyes first stir desire;
Your matchless wit, why fan the fire?
Repentance comes too late.

II.

Vain are the vows that you complain
Are to another fondly made;
All your advice to me's as vain;
You must not—cannot be obey'd;
My heart can't change, tho' you command,
Nor can my heart obey your hand,
Love's pow'r none can evade!

VERSES WRITTEN IN A GARDEN.

SEE how that pair of billing doves
With open murmurs own their loves;
And, heedless of censorious eyes,
Pursue their unpolluted joys:
No fears of future want molest
The downy quiet of their nest;
No int'rest join'd the happy pair,
Securely blest in Nature's care,
While her dear dictates they pursue;
For constancy is Nature too.

Can all the doctrine of our schools,
Our maxims, our religious rules,
Can learning, to our lives ensure
Virtue so bright, or bliss so pure?
The great Creator's happy ends
Virtue and pleasure ever blends:
In vain the church and court have try'd
Th' united essence to divide;
Alike they find their wild mistake,
The pedant priest, and giddy rake.

TRANSLATED BY HERSELF.

VOICI ces colombes lá que tu prends sur le fait,
Mepriser des passants le regard indiscret,
Sans cesser pour cela des momens le plus tendres,
L'un a l'autre se fair entendre,
Par les accens les plus touchans,
De leurs chastes ardeurs les signes eloquens,
Libres des soins d'un avenir sinistre
De la nature en repos dans le sein ;
Fideles à la loi de ce sage ministre
Il en fait la constance, et son active main,
De toute leur famille embrasse le destin,
De ce couple choisi nul interêt arbitre
De son servile doight n'en ourdit le lien.
O vous qui remplissés cette terrestre sphere,
Avec un ton de despoticité
Des accens de la verité,
Religion et morale austere,
Ecoles fites vous dans ce haut charactere ;
De vertu de felicite,
Faites vous des enfans de cette integrite.

La vertu de tout tems du bonheur indivise.
Tous deux par dieu sur un seul sceau tracés,
Malgré la cour malgre l'eglise,
Ne seront jamais devisés ;
Le prêtre avec son systeme rigide,
Le Protée en plaisir dans l'art volupteux,
Tous les deux vont enchainés a leur guide,
A la fatale erreur, le bandeau sur les yeux.

SONG.

FOND wishes you pursue in vain,
  My heart is vow'd away and gone;
Forbear thy sighs too lovely swain,
  Those dying airs that you put on!
Go try on other maids your art,
Ah! leave this lost unworthy heart,
  But you must leave it soon.

Such sighs as these you should bestow
  On some unpractis'd blooming fair;
Where rosy youth doth warmly glow,
  Whose eyes forbid you to despair.
Not all thy wond'rous charms can move
A heart, that must refuse your love,
  Or not deserve your care.

IMPROMPTU,

TO A YOUNG LADY SINGING.

SING gentle maid—reform my breast,
  And soften all my care;
Thus may I be some moments blest,
  And easy in despair.
The pow'r of Orpheus lives in you;
You can the passions of my soul subdue,
  And tame the lions and the tygers there.

ADVICE.

CEASE, fond shepherd—cease desiring
What you never must enjoy;
She derides your vain aspiring,
She to all your sex is coy.

Cunning Damon once pursu'd her,
Yet she never would incline;
Strephon too as vainly woo'd her,
Tho' his flocks are more than thine.

At Diana's shrine aloud,
By the zone around her waist,
Thrice she bow'd, and thrice she vow'd
Like the Goddess to be chaste.

ANSWER.

THO' I never got possession,
  'Tis a pleasure to adore ;
Hope, the wretch's only blessing,
  May in time procure me more.

Constant courtship may obtain her,
  Where both wealth and merit fail,
And the lucky minute gain her,
  Fate and fancy must prevail.

At Diana's shrine aloud,
  By the bow and by the quiver,
Thrice she bow'd and thrice she vow'd,
  Once to love—and that for ever.

EPISTLE TO LORD HERVEY,

ON THE KING'S BIRTH-DAY.

FROM THE COUNTRY,

Where I enjoy in contemplative chamber,
Lutes, laurels, seas of milk, and ships of amber.

THRO' shining crouds you now make way,
With sideling bow and golden key;
While wrapt in spleen and easy chair,
For all this pomp so small my care,
I scarce remember who are there.
Yet in brocade I can suppose,
The potent Knight,* whose presence goes
At least a yard before his nose;
And Majesty with sweeping train,
That does so many yards contain,
Superior to her waiting nymphs,
As lobster to attendant shrimps.
I do not ask one word of news,
Which country damsels much amuse.

* Sir Robert Walpole.

If a new batch of lords appears,
After a tour of half six years,
With foreign airs to grace the nation,
The Maids of Honour's admiration;
Whose bright improvements give surprise
To their own lady-mothers' eyes.
Improvements, such as colts might show,
Were mares so mad to let them go;
Their limbs perhaps a little stronger,
Their manes and tails grown somewhat longer.
I would not hear of ball-room scuffles,
Nor what new whims adorn the ruffles.
This meek epistle comes to tell,
On Monday, I in town shall dwell;
Where, if you please to condescend,
In Ca'endish-square, to see your friend,
I shall disclose to you alone
Such thoughts as ne'er were thought upon.

AN ANSWER TO A LADY,

WHO ADVISED LADY M. W. MONTĂGU TO RETIRE.

YOU little know the heart that you advise,
I view this various scene with equal eyes;
In crowded court I find myself alone,
And pay my worship to a nobler throne.

Long since the value of this world I knew;
Piti'd the folly, and despis'd the shew;
Well as I can, my tedious part I bear,
And wait dismissal without pain or fear.

Seldom I mark mankind's detested ways,
Not hearing censure nor affecting praise;
And unconcern'd my future fate I trust,
To that sole Being merciful and just.

WRITTEN AT LOUVERE,

OCTOBER, 1736.

IF age and sickness, poverty and pain,
Should each assault me with alternate plagues,
I know mankind is destined to complain,
And I submit to torment and fatigues.

The pious farmer, who ne'er misses pray'rs,
With patience suffers unexpected rain;
He blesses Heav'n for what its bounty spares,
And sees, resign'd, a crop of blighted grain.
But, spite of sermons, farmers would blaspheme,
If a star fell to set their thatch on flame.

CONCLUSION OF A LETTER TO A FRIEND,

SENT FROM ITALY, 1741.

BUT happy you from the contagion free,
Who, thro' her veil, can human nature see;
Calm you reflect, amid the frantic scene,
On the low views of those mistaken men
Who lose the short invaluable hour,
Thro' dirt-pursuing schemes of distant pow'r;
Whose best enjoyments never pay the chase,
But melt like snow within a warm embrace.
Believe me, friend, for such indeed are you,
Dear to my heart, and to my int'rest true;
Too much already have you thrown away,
Too long sustain'd the labour of the day:
Enjoy the remnant of declining light,
Nor wait for rest 'till overwhelm'd in night.
By present pleasure balance pain you've past,
Forget all systems, and indulge your taste.

TO THE SAME.

WHEREVER Fortune points my destin'd way,
If my capricious stars ordain my stay;
In gilded palace, or in rural scene,
While breath shall animate this frail machine.
My heart sincere, which never flatt'ry knew,
Shall consecrate its warmest wish to you.
A monarch compass'd by a suppliant croud,
Prompt to obey, and in his praises loud,
Among those thousands who on smiles depend,
Perhaps has no disinterested friend.

WRITTEN AT LOUVERE, 1755.

WISDOM, slow product of laborious years,
The only fruit that life's cold winter bears;
Thy sacred seeds in vain in youth we lay,
By the fierce storm of passion torn away.

Should some remain in a rich gen'rous soil,
They long lie hid, and must be rais'd with toil;
Faintly they struggle with inclement skies,
No sooner born than the poor planter dies.

ESSAYS

BY

Lady MARY WORTLEY MONTAGU.

PRINTED FROM HER ORIGINAL MANUSCRIPTS.

ESSAYS.

A LETTER

FROM THE OTHER WORLD, TO A LADY, FROM HER FORMER HUSBAND.

THIS Letter will surprize you less than it would any other of your sex; and therefore I think I need no apology in breaking through a rule of good-breeding, which has been observed so strictly by all husbands, for so many ages, who, however troublesome while they lived, have never frightened their wives by the least notice of them after their deaths; but your reverend Doctor will inform you that there is nothing supernatural in this correspondence; and that the existence of immortal spirits includes a tender concern for the poor militant mortals of your world. I own I was a little puzzled how to convey this epistle, and thought it best to assume a material form for some few moments, and put it myself into the Penny-post. In my hurry (being very impatient to let you hear from me) I unluckily forgot my little finger, which produced an odd accident; for the wench at the Post-office would have taken me up for one of the incendiaries. Already had the mob assembled round the door, and nothing but dissolving into air, could have saved me from Newgate. Several run down the allies in pursuit of me; and particular care was taken of my letter, in hopes of reading it, in the Newspaper. You may imagine I would not have exposed myself to this adventure, but out of the sincerest regard to the happiness of the dear partner of my worldly cares. Without the least uneasiness I have seen you dispose of yourself into the arms of another; and I would never disturb you while you were seeking pleasure in forgetting me; but I cannot bear that you should constrain yourself out of respect to me. I see every motion of your mind now much clearer than I did in my life, (though then I guessed pretty shrewdly sometimes) I know the real content that you find in pink-coloured ribbon, and am sensible how much you sacrifice to imaginary decency every time you put on that odious rusty black, which is half worn out. Alas! my dear Eliza, in these seats of perfect love and beauty, the veriest scrub of a Cherubim, (some of which have raked cinders behind Montagu-house, as they often tell me) is more charming than you were, on your first wedding-day. Judge, then, whether I can have any satisfaction in looking at your crape hood, when I am in this bright company. You know that in my terrestrial state, three bottles would sometimes raise me to that pitch of philosophy, I utterly forgot you, when you were but some few inches from me. Do not fancy me grown so impertinent here, as to observe so nicely whether you obey the forms of widowhood; and do not think to cajole me with such instances of your affection, when you are giving the most substantial proofs of it, to another man. I have already assured you I am exalted above jealousy, if I could have been sensible of it. You have provoked me by a second choice, so absolutely opposite to your first. He is often talking of certain fellows he calls Classic Authors, who I never troubled my head with; and I know this letter will meet with more regard from him than from you, for he is better skilled in the language of the dead than the living.

ESSAY IN A PAPER, CALLED THE NONSENSE OF COMMON SENSE.

PUBLISHED JANUARY 24, 1738.

I HAVE always, as I have already declared, profeſſed myself a friend, tho' I do not aspire to the character of an admirer, of the fair sex; and as such, I am warmed with indignation at the barbarous treatment they have received from the *Common Sense* of *January* 14, and the false advice that he gives them. He either knows them very little, or, like an interested quack, prescribes such medicines as are likely to hurt their constitutions. It is very plain to me, from the extreme partiality with which he speaks of *Operas*, and the rage with which he attacks both *Tragedy* and *Comedy*, that the author is a *Performer* in the *Opera*: and whoever reads his paper with attention, will be of my opinion: else no *thing* alive would aſſert at the same time the innocence of an entertainment, contrived wholly to soften the mind and sooth the sense, without any pretence to a moral; and so vehemently declaim against plays, whose end is, to shew the fatal consequence of vice, to warn the innocent against the snares of a well-bred designing *Dorimant.* You see there to what insults a woman of wit, beauty, and quality is exposed, that has been seduced by the artificial tenderness of a vain, agreeable gallant; and, I believe, that very comedy has given more checks to ladies in pursuit of present pleasures, so closely attended with shame and sorrow, than all the sermons they have ever heard in their lives. But this author does not seem to think it possible to ſtop their propensity to gallantry by reason or reflection. He only desires them to fill up their time with all sorts of trifles: in short, he recommends to them gossiping, scandal, lying, and a whole troop of follies, inſtead of it, as the only preservatives for their virtue.

I am for treating them with more dignity;

and, as I profess myself a protector of all the oppressed, I shall look upon them as my peculiar care. I expect to be told, this is downright *Quixotism*, and that I am venturing to engage the strongest part of mankind, with a paper helmet upon my head. I confess it is an undertaking where I cannot foresee any considerable success, and, according to an author I have read somewhere,

> The world will still be rul'd by knaves,
> And fools, contending to be slaves.

But however, I keep up to the character of a moralist, and shall use my endeavours to relieve the distressed, and defeat vulgar prejudices, whatever the event may be. Among the most universal errors, I reckon that of treating the weaker sex with a contempt, which has a very bad influence on their conduct. How many of them think it excuse enough to say they are women, to indulge any folly that comes into their heads? This renders them useless members of the common-wealth, and only burdensome to their own families, where the wise husband thinks he lessens the opinion of his own understanding, if he at any time condescends to consult his wife's. Thus what reason nature has given them is thrown away, and a blind obedience expected from them by all their ill-natured masters; and, on the other side, as blind a complaisance shown by those that are indulgent, who say often, that women's weakness must be complied with, and it is a vain troublesome attempt to make them hear reason.

I attribute a great part of this way of thinking, which is hardly ever controverted, either to the ignorance of authors, who are many of them heavy *Collegians*, that have never been admitted to politer conversations than those of their *bed-makers*, or to the design of selling their works, which is generally the only view of writing, without any regard to truth, or the ill-consequences that attend the propagation of wrong notions. A paper smartly wrote, though perhaps only some old conceits dressed in new words, either in rhime or prose: I say *rhime*, for I have seen no *verses* wrote for many years. Such a paper, either to ridicule or declaim against the ladies, is very welcome to the coffee-houses, where there is hardly one man in ten, but fancies he hath some reason or other to curse some of the sex most heartily. Perhaps his sisters' fortunes are to run away with the money that would be better bestowed at the Groom-porter's; or an old mother, good for nothing, keeps a jointure from a hopeful son, that wants to make a settlement on his mistress; or a handsome young fellow is plagued with a wife, that will remain alive, to hinder his running away with a great fortune, having two or three of them in love with him. These are serious misfortunes, that are sufficient to exasperate the mildest tempers to a contempt of the sex; not to speak of lesser inconveniences, which are very provoking at the time they are felt.

How many pretty gentlemen have been unmercifully jilted by pert hussies, after having curtesied to them at *half a dozen Operas*; nay permitted themselves to be led out *twice*: yet, after these encouragements, which amount very near to an engagement, have refused to read their *billets-doux*, and perhaps married other men, under their noses. How welcome is a couplet or two, in scorn of womankind, to such a disappointed lover; and with what comfort he reads, in many profound authors, that they are never to be pleased but by *coxcombs*? and, consequently, he owes his ill success to the brightness of his understanding, which is beyond female comprehension. The country 'squire is confirmed in the elegant choice he has made, in preferring the conversation of his hounds to that of his wife; and the kind keepers, a numerous sect, find themselves justified in throwing away their time and estates on a parcel of jilts, when they read, that neither birth nor education can make any of the sex rational creatures; and they can have no value, but what is to be ſeen in their faces.

Hence ſprings the applause with which such libels are read; but I would ask the applauders, if these notions, in their own nature, are likely to produce any good effect towards reforming the *vicious*, instructing the weak, or guiding the young? I would not every day tell my footmen, if I kept any, that their whole fraternity were a pack of scoundrels—that lying and stealing were inseparable qualities from their cloth—that I should think myself very happy in them, if they confined themselves to innocent lies, and would only steal candles'-ends. On the contrary, I would say in their presence, that birth and money were accidents of fortune, that no man was to be seriously despised for wanting them; that an honest faithful servant was a character of more value than an insolent corrupt lord; that the real distinction between man and man lay in his integrity, which, in one shape or other, generally met with its reward in the world, and could not fail of giving the highest pleasure, by a consciousness of virtue, which every man feels, that is so happy to possess it.

With this gentleness would I treat my inferiors, with much greater esteem would I speak to that beautiful half of mankind, who are distinguished by *petticoats*. If I were a divine I would remember, that in their first creation they were designed as a help for the other sex, and nothing was ever made incapable of the end of its creation. 'Tis true, the first lady had so little experience that she hearkened to the persuasion of an impertinent dangler; and if you mind, he succeeded by persuading her that she was not so wise as she should be.

Men that have not sense enough to shew any superiority in their arguments, hope to be yielded to by a faith, that as they are men, all the reason that has been allotted to human kind, has fallen to their share. I am seriously of another opinion. As much greatness of mind may be shewn in submission as in command;

and some women have suffered a life of hardships with as much philosophy as *Cato* traversed the desarts of *Africa*, and without that support the view of glory offered him, which is enough for the human mind that is touched with it, to go through any toil or danger. But this is not the situation of a woman, whose virtue must only shine to her own recollection, and loses that name when it is ostentatiously exposed to the world. A lady who has performed her duty as a daughter, a wife, and a mother, raises in me as much veneration as *Socrates* or *Xenophon*; and much more than I would pay either to *Julius Cæsar* or *Cardinal Mazarine*, tho' the first was the most famous enslaver of his country, and the last the most successful plunderer of his master.

A woman really virtuous, in the utmost extent of this expression, has virtue of a purer kind than any philosopher has ever shewn; since she knows, if she has sense, and without it there can be no virtue, that mankind is too much prejudiced against her sex, to give her any degree of that fame which is so sharp a spur to their great actions. I have some thoughts of exhibiting a set of pictures of such meritorious ladies, where I shall say nothing of the fire of their eyes, or the pureness of their complexions; but give them such praises as befits a rational sensible being: virtues of choice, and not beauties of accident. I beg they would not so far mistake me, as to think I am undervaluing their charms: a beautiful mind in a beautiful body, is one of the finest objects shewn us by nature. I would not have them place so much value on a quality that can be only useful to one, as to neglect that which may be of benefit to thousands, by precept or by example. There will be no occasion of amusing them with trifles, when they consider themselves capable of not only making the most amiable but the most estimable figures in life. Begin then ladies, by paying those authors with scorn and contempt, who, with a sneer of affected admiration, would throw you below the dignity of the human species.

CARABOSSE

A L'ABBE' CONTI.

IL y avoit autrefois un Prince & une Princesse (car c'est ainsi que ma nourice commençoit tous les contes dont elle me berçoit). Le Prince estoit brave & genereux, la Princesse belle & sage: leurs vertus, & leur amour reciproque & constant faisoient toute à la fois la gloire & la honte du siecle. Mais comme il n'y a point de felicité parfaite, il leur manquoit des enfans: les temples de tout les dieux estoient chargés de leurs offrandes, & toutes les bonnes fées des environs de leur presents, pour obtenir la seule chose qu'ils avoient à souhaiter. Il y est vrai qu'on ne pût jamais persuader a la Princesse de rechercher les mauvaises & c'éstoit en vain que le Prince lui representoit que les mechantes pouvoient nuire avec autant de facilité que les bienfaisantes pouvoient servir; elle disoit toujours que faire la cour aux vicieux, estoit une espece de culte rendue au vice, & elle ne pouvoit pas s'y resoudre. On dit même qu'elle s'emancipoit quelquefois a blamer leur conduite d'une façon un peu temeraire. Enfin ses veux furent comblé, elle devint grosse, elle n'oublia pas de prier à ses couches toutes les fées de ses amies, et elle leur preparoit de presents digne de leur estre offerte. Donner de Pierreries ou de l'or aux maitresses des mines, auroit été leur faire un affront, elle sçavoit qu'elles en font si peu de cas qu'elles en comblent souvent les mortels les plus indignes pour en mieux marquer leur mepris. Elle avoit ramassé par les soins infinis Des beaux vers passionés composoient par des amants sinceres, le portrait d'une belle religieuse qui n'avoit jamais pensé à l'amour profane, une phiole (tres petite a la verité) des larmes verésés par une jeune & riche veuve seule dans son cabinet, & des livres de theologie qui n'avoient jamais ennuyé personne. Les fées etoient toutes etonnes d'où elle auroit pû trouver tant de choses rares & precieuse ; elles etoient empressés de temoigner leur reconnoisance en rendant son enfant la personne du monde la plus accomplie & la plus heureuse. Elle mit au monde une petite Princesse : a peine avoit elle vû la lumiere que la fée Bellinde s'écria, Je la doue d'une beauté noble & touchante. Elle n'avoit pas cessée de parler quand on entendoit un bruit comme de cent connons déclargés à la fois, un sifflement comme de mille serpents furieux, & on vit descendre par la cheminée la Fée Carabosse, montée à califoorchon sur un enorme crapaud. Je ne veux salir mon papier par la description de sa figure, faitte pour inspirer le degout et l'horreur. Je veux (crioit-elle d'une voix rauque) que cette Fille cherie perde cette beauté admirable par la petite verole dans l'age qu'elle commence à sentir ses avantages. La Fée Spirituelle, se flattant d'adoucir cet malheur, disoit, Je la doûe d'une memoire la plus heureuse qui a jamais été, d'un goût juste, d'une vivacité surprenante, tempérée par un jugement qui reglera toutes ses paroles ; elle excellera dans tous les genres d'écrire, elle seroit sçavante sans vanité, & vive sans etourderie. Cet bel esprit (repliqua Carabosse avec un souris dédaigneux) ne servira qu'à lui attirer les ennemis, elle seroit toujours en proye aux sots, dechirée par leurs mallices, & importunée par leurs assiduités. Je veux, dissoit la brillante Argentine en s'avançant, que son Pere soit le plus riche Seigneur de son rang, & que son mari auroit des millions d'or. Oui, interrompit Carabosse, elle vivra au milieu des trésors sans en voir jamais à sa disposition. Je lui donne, disoit Hygeia, une santé à toute épreuve, que ni les chagrins ni les fatigues ne pourront diminuer. Cette santé repondit Carabosse, lui inspirera la hardiesse de tenter des enterprises temeraires, & de risquer des dangers dout elle seroit toujours environnés. Elle aura, disoit l'aimable Harmonie, l'oreille juste & un goût exquis pour la musique—Je lui oste (crioit Carabosse en lui coupant la parole) le pouvoir de chanter, pour qu'elle sente tout la rage du desir & de l'impuissance. Les bonnes fées, consterneés de voir leur benedictions ainsi empoisonceés, se parloient tout bas, & consultoient en quelle maniere on pouvoit vaincre cette malice infernale. Spirituelle crût avoir trouvée un expedient infaillible : il faut lui oster (disoit elle) toutes les vices, & elle se trouvera garentie des malheurs qui en sont la suitte. Je lui oste (ajouta-elle d'un ton haut & ferme) toutes les semences de l'envie, & de l'avarice, qui sont les sources des miseres de l'humanité ; elle aura l'humeur douce et egalle,—& un grand fond le tendresse, s'ecria Cabarosse avec un éclat de rire que faisoit trembler le Palais.—Les Fées bienfaisantes s'envolerent, nevoiant aucune remede à tant des maux. La Princesse mourût de chagrin, son enfant s'embellisoit chaque jour ; mais - - - - ici le manuscript est deffecteux.

SUR LA

MAXIME DE M. ROCHEFOUCAULT.

QU'IL Y A DES MARRIAGES COMMODES, MAIS POINT DE DELICIEUX.

IL paroist bien hardi d'entreprendre de detruire une maxime etablie par un bel esprit si celebre que Mr. de Rochefoûcault, et receu avec un joy si aveugle chez une nation, qui se dit la seule parfeitement polie du monde, et qui a donnée depuis si long temps des loix de galanterie à toute l'Europe.

Cependant (plein de l'ardeur qu'inspire la verité) j'ose avancer tout le contraire, et je soutiens hardiment, qu'il n'y a qu'un amour marié qui peut etre delicieux pour une ame bien faite.

La nature nous a presentée des plaisirs propre pour notre espece, on n'a qu'a suivre son instinct rafiné pour le goût, et relevé par une imagination vive et douce, pour trouver le seul bonheur dont les mortels sont capables. L'ambition, l'avarice, la vanité, ne peuvent donner (dans leurs plus grandes jouissances) que de plaisirs bas, mediocres, et qui ne sont pas capables de toucher un cœur noble.

On peut regarder les bienfaits de la fortune, comme des echaffauts necessaires pour monter au bonheur, mais on ne peut jamais le trouver, soit en y bornant ses souhaites, soit en obtenant ses frivoles saveures, qui ne sont que les gênes de la vie, quand on le regarde pas comme necessaire pour obtenir ou conserver, une felicité plus precieuse. Cette felicité ne se trouve que dans l'amitié fondée sur un estime parfait fixé par la reconnoissance, soutenu par l'inclination, et eveillé par la tendresse de l'amour, que les anciens ont tres bien depeints sous la figure d'un bel enfant; il se plait dans les jeux enfantins, il est tendre et delicat, incapable de nuire, charmé des bagatelles, tous ses desseins se terminent en des plaisirs, mais ces plaisirs sont doux et innocents. On a representé, sous un figure bien different une autre passion trop gros pour nommer (mais dont le pluspart d'hommes sont seulement capable.) Je veux dire celui d'un satyr, qui est plus bestial qu'humain, et on a exprimé dans cet animal equivoque le vicè & la brutalité de cet appetit sensuel, qui est cependant le vrai fondement de tous les beaux procedés de la belle galanterie. Une passion, qui tache de s'assouvir, dans la perte de ce qu'elle trouve de plus aimable au monde, qui est fondé sur l'injustice, soutenue par la tromperie, et suivie des crimes, de remors, de la honte, et du mepris, peut elle etre delicieux pour un cœur vertueux? Voila pourtant l'aimable equipage de tous les engagements illegitimes; on se trouve obligé d'arracher de l'ame; tous les sentimens de l'honneur inseparable d'une education noble, et de vivre miserable dans la poursuite eternelle de ce qu'on condamne, d'avoir tous ses plaisirs empoisoné de remors, et d'être reduit à cet etat malheureux de renoncer à la vertu sans pouvoir se plaire dans le vice.

On ne peut gouter les douceurs d'un amour parfait, que dans une mariage bien assortie : rien ne marque tant de petitesse dans l'esprit, que de s'arrester aux paroles. Qu'importe que la coutume (pour laquelle nous voions d'assez bonnes raisons) a donné un peu de ridicule a ces paroles, de mari et de femme ? Un mari signifi (dans l'interpretration generale) un jaloux, brutal, grondeur, tyran, ou bien un bon sot, a qui on peut tout imposer : une femme est un demon domestique, qu'on donne pour tromper ou pour tourmenter ce pauvre homme. La conduite de la pluspart des gens justifie assez ces deux caracteres, mais encore, qu'importe de paroles ? un mariage bien reglé ne ressemble pas à ces mariages d'interest ou d'ambition ; ce sont deux amants, qui vivent ensemble : qu'un prestre dit de certains paroles, qu'un notaire signe de certains papiers, je regarde ces preparatifs dans la même vue, qu'un amant l'echelle de corde, qu'il attache à la fenestre de sa maitresse.

Pourvu qu'on vive ensemble, qu'importe à quel prix & par quelles moiens?

Il est impossible, qu'un amour parfait et bien fondé soit heureux que dans la paisible possession de l'objet aimé, et cette paix, n'oste rien de la douceur ni de la vivacité d'une passion telle que je sai l'imaginer. Si je voulois m'occuper a faire des Romans, je ne voudrois pas placer les images du vrai bonheur dans l'Arcadie, ni sur le bords de Lignon; je ne suis pas assez precieuse pour borner la plus delicate tendresse à des souhaits. Je commencerais le Roman par le mariage de deux personnes unies par l'esprit, par le gout, et par l'inclination. Se peut-il donc rien de plus heureux, que d'unir leurs interests, et leurs jours? L'Amant a le plaisir de donner la derniere marque d'estime et de confiance à sa maitresse, et l'Amante lui donne en recompense le soin de son repos et de sa liberté. Peut-on se donner des gages plus chers ou plus tendres! et n'est-il pas naturel de souhaiter de donner de preuves incontestables d'une tendresse dont l'ame est penetré ?

Je sai, qu'il y a des faux delicats, qui soutiennes que les plaisirs de l'amour ne sont dues, qu'aux difficultés et aux dangers. Ils disent fort spirituellement, que la rose ne seroit pas rose, sans espines, et mille fadaises de cette nature, qui font si peu d'impression sur mon esprit, que je suis persuadé, que si j'etois Amant, la crainte de nuire à celle que j'aimerois, me rendroit malheureux, si sa possession meme étoit accompagné des dangers pour elle.

La vie des amans mariés est bien differente; ils ont le plaisir de la passer dans une suite d'obligations mutuelles, & des marques de bienveillance, & on a la joye de voir qu'on fait le bonheur entier de l'objet aimé, en quel point je place la joüisance parfaite.

Les plus petits soins de le l'œconomie deviennent nobles & delicats, quand ils sont relevés par des sentimens de tendresse. Meubler une chambre n'est pas meubler une chambre, ce'st orner un lieu où j'attends mon Amant ; ordonner un souper, n'est pas simplement donner des ordres a mon cuisinier, c'est m'amuser à regaler celui que j'aime : ces occupations necessaires regardés, dans cette vûe par une personne amoureuse, sont des plaisirs mille fois plus vifs & plus touchant que les spectacles & le jeu, qui font le bonheur de cette foule incapable de la vraie volupté. Une passion heureuse & contente adoucit tous les mouvemens de l'ame, & dore tous les objets qu'on voit. Un Amant heureux (j'entends marié à sa maitresse) s'il exerce une charge, les fatigues d'un camp, l'embarras d'une cour, tout lui devient agréable, quand c'est pour servir celle qu'il aime. Si la fortune favorable (car cela ne depend nullement du merite) fait reüsir ses desseins, tous les avantages qu'elle lui donnent, sont des offrandes qu'il met aux pieds de sa charmante amie, il la remercie de l'inspiration qu'il doit à ses charmes, & il trouve dans le succes de son ambition, un plaisir plus vif, & plus digne d'un honnête homme, que celui d'élever sa fortune, & d'être applaudi du public. Il joüit de la gloire, du rang, & de la richesse, que par rapport à celle qu'il aime, & c'est son amant qu'il entend louer, quand il s'attire l'approbation d'un parlement, l'applaudissement d'un armée, ou l'agrément de son prince. Dans le malheur c'est son consolation de se retirer, aupres d'une personne attendrie par ses disgraces, & de se dire entre ses bras, Mon bonheur ne dépend pas la caprice de la fortune, ici j'ai un azile asseuré contre les chagrins, vostre estime me rende insensible à l'injustice d'une cour, ou à l'ingratitude d'un maitre, & j'ai un espece de plaisir dans la perte de mon bien, puisque cette infortune me donne de nouvelles preuves de vostre tendresse. A quoi servent les grandeurs à des personnes deja heureuses? Nous n'avons besoin ni des flatteurs ni des equipages, je regne dans vostre cœur, & je possede toutes les delices de la nature dans vostre personne.

Enfin il n'y a point de situation dont la tristesse n'est pas capable d'être diminuée par la compagnie de l'objet de son amour; une maladie mesme n'est pas sans douceurs, quand on a le sir d'être soignée par celle qu'on aime. Je ne finirai jamais, si j'entreprenois de donner une detail de tous les agrémens d'une union où l'on trouve à la fois, tout ce que peut satisfaire un imagination tendre & delicat, & tout ce qui flatte les sens dans la volupté la plus pure & la plus étendue; mais je ne sçaurois finir sans parler du plaisir de voir croitre tous les jours, les aimables marques d'une tendre amitié, & de s'occuper (selon leur differens sexes) à les perfectioner. On s'abandonne à cet doux instinct de la nature, raffiné par l'amour. On baisse dans une fille la beauté de sa mere, & on respecte dans un fils l'esprit & les apparences d'une probité naturelle qu'on estime dans son pere. C'est un plaisir auquel Dieu mesme (à ce que dit Moïse) a été sensible, quand voiant ce qu'il avoit fait, il le trouvoit bon. A propos de Moïse, le premier plan du bonheur, a infiniment surpassé tous les autres, & je ne sçaurois former d'idée d'un Paradis plus Paradis que l'état où étoient placés nos premiers parens. Cela n'a pas duré parcequ'ils ne connoissoient pas le monde, & c'est par la mesme raison, qu'on voit si peu des mariages d'inclination heureux. Eve étoit une sotte enfant, et Adam un homme fort peu eclairé: quand des gens de cet espece se rencontrent ils ont beau estre amoureux, cela ne peut pas durer. Ils se forment pendant la fureur de leur amour des idées surnaturelles; un homme croit sa maitresse une ange parce qu'elle est belle, et une femme est enchanté du merite de son amant parce qu'il l'adore. Le premier changement de son teint lui oste son adoration, et le mari cessant d'être adorateur devient haïsable, à celle qui n'a pas eû d'autre fondement de son amour. Ils se degoutent peu à peu, et à l'exemple de nos premiers parens ils ne manquent pas de rejetter l'un sur l'autre le crime de leur mutuelle foiblesse. Après la froideur, le mepris marche à grand pas, et il sont prevenus, qu'il faut se haïr puis qu'ils sont mariés. Leurs moindres defauts se grossissent à leur veue, et ils sont aveugles sur les agrémens, qui pourroient leur toucher en tout autre personne. Un commerce etabli sur l'usage du sens, ne peut pas avoir d'autre suite. Un homme en epousant sa maitresse doit oublier qu'elle lui paroist adorable, pour considerer que c'est une simple mortelle sujete aux maladies, aux caprices, et à la mauvaise humeur: il doit preparer sa constance à soutenir la perte, de sa beauté, et amasser un fonds de complaisance, qui est necessaire pour la conversation continuelle de la personne du monde la plus raisonable et la moins inegale. La dame de son coté, ne droit pas attendre une suite des flatteries et d'obeissance, elle se doit disposer elle-même à obeir agreablement, science très difficile, et par consequence d'un grand merite auprès d'un homme capable de le sentir. Elle doit tacher de relever les charmes d'une maitresse par le bon sens et la solidité d'une amie. Quand deux personnes préoccupées par de sentimens si raisonables, sont uni par des liens eternels, la nature entiere leur rit, et les objets les plus communs leur deviennent charmans. Il me semble, que c'est une vie infiniment plus douce, plus elegante, et plus volupteuse, que la galanterie la plus heureuse et la mieux conduite. Une femme capable de reflexion ne peut regarder un amant autrement qu'un seducteur, qui veut profiter de sa foiblesse pour se donner un plaisir d'un moment, aux dépens de sa gloire, de son repos, et peut-être de sa vie. Un voleur, qui met le pistolet à la gorge pour enlever une bourse me paroist plus honnête, et moins coupable; et j'ai assez bonne opinion de moi pour croire, que si j'étois homme, je serois aussi capable de former le plan d'un assassinat, que celui de corrompre une honnete femme, estimée dans le monde et heureuse dans son ménage. Serois-je capable d'empoisonner son cœur en lui inspirant une passion funeste, à laquelle il faut immoler l'honneur, la tranquillité, et la vertu? Rendrois-je meprisable une personne parce quelle me paroist aimable? dois-je recompenser sa tendresse en lui rendant sa maison en horreur, ses enfans indifférens, et son mari detesté. Je croique ces reflexions me paroistroient dans la même force si mon sexe m'avoit rendu excusable dans de pareils procedés, et j'espere, que j'aurois été assez sensé pour ne pas croire le vice moins vicieux, parce qu'il est à la mode.

J'estime beaucoup les mœurs Turcs, (peuple ignorant, mais tres poli à ma fantaisie.) Un galant convaincu d'avoir debauché une femme mariée est regardée parmi eux, avec le même horreur qu'une dame abandonée chez nous. Il est sure de ne jamais faire fortune, et on auroit honte de donner un charge considerable à un homme soupçonné d'avoir faite une injustice si enorme. Que dir-t-on dans cette nation morale si on voyoit quelques uns de nos Anti-chevaliers-errans, qui sont toujours en poursuite d'aventures pour mettre des filles innocentes en détresse, et pour perdre l'honneur des femmes de condition? qui ne regardent la beauté, la jeunesse, le rang et la vertu même, que comme des aiguillons pour exciter le desir de les ruiner? et qui mettent toute leure gloire à paroistre des seducteurs habiles; oubliant qu'avec tous leurs soins ils ne peuvent jamais atteindre qu'au second rang de ce bel escadron, les diables ayant été depuis si long temps en possession du premier? J'avoue, que nos manieres barbares sont si bien calculées pour l'etablissement du vice et du malheur (qui en est inseparable), qu'il faut avoir des têtes et des cœurs infiniment au-dessus du commun, pouvoir jouïr de la felicité d'un mariage tel que je viens de le depeindre. La nature est si foible et si portée au changement, qu'il est difficile de soutenir la constance le mieux fondée parmi toutes les dissipations que nos coutumes ridicules ont rendu inevitables. Un mari amoureux a peine à voir prendre à sa femme toutes les libertés du bel usage: il paroist y avoir de la dureté à les refuser: et il se trouve reduit, pour se conformer aux manieres polies de l'Europe, de voir tous les jours ses mains en proye à qui les veut prendre, de l'entendre partager à toute la terre les charmes de son esprit, la voir montrer sa gorge en plein midi, se parer pour des bals et des spectacles, s'attirer des adorateurs, et ecouter les fades flatteries de mille et mille sots. Peut-on soutenir son estime pour une creature si publique? et ne perd elle pas (au moins) beaucoup de son prix? Je reviens toujours à mes manieres Orientales, où les plus belles femmes, se contentent de limiter le pouvoir de leurs charmes, à celui à qui il est permis d'en joüir: elles ont trop d'humanité pour souhaiter de faire des miserables, et elles sont trop sinceres, pour ne pas avouer qu'elles se croient capable d'exciter des passions.

Je me souviens d'une conversation que j'ai eûe avec une dame de grande qualité à Constantinople (la plus aimable femme que j'ai connue de ma vie, et pour qui j'ai eûe en suite, une tendre amitié): elle m'avoua naïvement qu'elle étoit contente de son mari. Que vous êtes libertines (me disoit-elle), vous autres dames Chretiennes! il vous est permis, de recevoir les visites d'autant d'hommes que vous voulez, et vos loix vous permettent sans bornes, l'usage de l'amour et du vin. Je l'assurai qu'elle estoit fort mal instruite ; qu'il estoit vrai que nous recevions des visites, mais ces visites etoient plein du respect et du retenu, et que c'estoit une crime d'entendre parler d'amour, ou d'aimer un autre que son mari. Vos maris sont bien bons (me repliqua-t-elle en riant) de se contenter d'une fidelité si bornée : vos yeux, vos mains, vostre conversation, est pour le publique, et que pretendez-vous reserver pour eux ? Pardonnez-moi, ma belle Sultane, (ajouta-t-elle en m'embrassant ;) j'ai toute l'inclination possible de croire tout ce que vous me dites, mais vous voulez m'imposer des impossibilités. Je sçai les saletés des infidelles ; je voye que vous en avez honte, et je ne vous en parlerai plus.

J'ai trouvé tant de bon sens et de vraisemblance en tout ce qu'elle me disoit, que j'avois peine à la contredire ; et j'avouai d'abord qu'elle avoit raison de preferer les mœurs Mussulmans à nos coûtumes ridicules, qui sont une confusion surprenante des maximes severes de la Christianisme avec toute la libertinage des Lacedemoniennes : et nonobstant nos folles manieres, je suis du sentiment qu'une femme determinée faire son bonheur de l'amour de son mari, doit abandonner le desir extravagant de se faire adorer du public ; et qu'un mari qui aime tendrement sa femme, doit se priver de la reputation d'être galant à la cour. Vous voyez que je suppose deux personnes bien extraordinaires : il n'est pas donc fort surprenant, qu'un tel union soit bien rare, dans les païs où il est necessaire de mepriser les coûtumes les plus etablies, pour être heureux.

GENERAL INDEX.

A.

B.

C.

D.

E.

F.

G.

H.

I.

L.

M.

N.

O.

P.

Q.

R.

S.

T.

THE END.

Printed by J. Adlard, Duke-street, Smithfield.

Made in the USA
San Bernardino, CA
09 July 2013